M. K. Gandhi's First Nonviolent Campaign

M. K. GANDHI'S FIRST NONVIOLENT CAMPAIGN

A Study of Racism in South Africa and the United States

George Hendrick and Willene Hendrick

AMHERST, NEW YORK

Copyright 2013 George Hendrick and Willene Hendrick

All rights reserved
Printed in the United States of America

No part of this publication may be reproduced, stored in or introduced into a retrieval system, or transmitted, in any form, or by any means (electronic, mechanical, photocopying, recording, or otherwise), without the prior permission of the publisher.

Requests for permission should be directed to:
permissions@teneopress.com, or mailed to:
Teneo Press
PO Box 350
Youngstown, NY 14174

Library of Congress Control Number: 2013943897

Hendrick, George and Hendrick, Willene.
M.K. Gandhi's First Nonviolent Campaign: A Study of Racism in South Africa and in the United States.
p. cm.
Includes bibliographical references.
ISBN 978-1-934844-91-5 (alk. paper).

Table of Contents

Preface vii

Introduction ix

Chapter I: Before South Africa 1

Chapter II: Before South Africa 17

Chapter III: Gandhi Faces Racism in South Africa 31

Chapter IV: Gandhi's Early Experiences in Natal 57

Chapter V: Gandhi and the Ultimate in Racism 69

Chapter VI: The Transvaal and Racism 95

Chapter VII: Gandhi Acquires *Indian Opinion* 117

Chapter VIII: Love 137

Chapter IX: Smuts's Betrayal and the Consequences 143

Chapter X: The Satyagraha Movement Saved by Justice Searle 165

Chapter XI: Nonviolence Succeeded but Racism Remained 181

Bibliography 201

Index 205

About the Authors 211

Preface

Willene Lowery Hendrick had a fatal heart attack just as we completed Chapter V. I have now finished the manuscript using the outline we had agreed upon. Sarah Jourdain helped with computer searches.

Librarians at the University of Illinois at Urbana-Champaign and the Urbana Free Library assisted in many ways, including Interlibrary Loans.

> **rac·ism** *n* **1** A doctrine or teaching, without scientific support, that claims to find racial differences in character, intelligence, etc., that asserts the superiority of one race over another or others, and that seeks to maintain the supposed purity of a race or the races **2** any program or practice of racial discrimination, segregation, etc. based on such beliefs.
> —Webster's New World Dictionary

Introduction

Until M. K. Gandhi (1869–1948) left India for London in 1888, he lived the sheltered life of a younger son of a prime minister of a princely state. Gandhi's father had learned how to survive in colonial India controlled by the British and their minions, the local princes. Young Gandhi was a dutiful son, but he had conflicting views about the Raj (the British government which dominated India); he supported it but was also aware that India was ruled by a foreign power.

Most officials in the Raj believed in white supremacy and were thorough racists. Many Indians were aware of those feelings of superiority shown by British officials, and they found it galling to be ruled by outsiders who felt the ruled should adapt Western ways and customs. In high school, though, Gandhi was introduced to Western thinking, especially English language, literature, and culture, and for many years he was a true believer.

To educated Indians, Queen Victoria, who became Empress of India in 1876, appeared to be a beacon of hope. In 1858, she promised Indians the same privileges and protections of all her subjects. She had been opposed to slavery, and she disapproved of disparagement of people of color. She forced Lord Salisbury to apologize for his reference to Indians as "black men."[1] In 1898, she wrote to the Viceroy, Lord Curzon, that he must shake himself free from his "narrow minded Council" and "overbearing officials" and *"hear for himself* what the feelings of the Natives really are." She warned against trampling on Indians making them *"feel* that they are a conquered people." She wanted the British to remain in control of densely-populated India, but Indians should recognize that the British were masters. This control, she believed "should be done kindly and not offensively," as had often been the case in the past.[2]

Empress Victoria showed in this letter that she was a compassionate Imperialist, but an Imperialist never-the-less. She believed that India should be ruled by the Raj; she thought that Indians were not capable of self-rule. What she did not fully understand was that arrogant, overbearing British officials often trampled on Indians. She wanted Indians to know in a kindly fashion that the British were masters. The Raj serving her were often intolerant, scornful of Indian religions, and only semi-humane. She never travelled to India and did not know the full extent of problems between the Raj and the Indian subjects. Indian schoolchildren, including Gandhi, had stirrings of resentment, but were also admirers of British culture.

****

At this same period of Gandhi's early life, the conditions for blacks in the United States improved for a short time. During the Civil War, slaves were emancipated, and after the end of the war in 1865 the ruling Republicans in Congress began to give additional rights to black people. The Fourteenth Amendment to the Constitution, ratified in 1868, declared, "All persons born or naturalized in the United States, and subject to the jurisdiction thereof, are citizens of the United States and of the state wherein they live." The amendment continued, "No State shall make or enforce any law which shall abridge the privileges or immunities of citizens of the United States...." The Fifteenth Amendment, ratified in 1870, declared specifically, "The right of citizens of the United States to vote shall not be denied or abridged by the United States or by any State on account of race,

Introduction

color, or previous condition of servitude."[3] The intent of the amendment is absolutely clear, but most Southerners, in public and privately, had deep reservations about both amendments.

During the twelve years of Reconstruction, 1865–1877, blacks began to vote and hold elective office, schools for blacks were established, and public transportation was less segregated. Large numbers of white people were actively opposed to the newly-gained rights of black people; they refused to send their children to schools that were not segregated. The Ku Klux Klan and other similar white-supremacist organizations began to intimidate and murder blacks to keep them voting and to "keep them in their place."

The racist attitude of whites was bluntly expressed by Benjamin F. Perry, provisional governor of South Carolina, in 1865: "The African has been in all ages, a savage or a slave. God created him inferior to the white men in form, color, and intellect, and no legislation or culture can make him his equal....God created differences between the two races, and nothing can make him equal."[4]

With the end of Reconstruction on 1877, the South moved quickly to nullify the newly-gained rights of blacks and to enact discriminatory laws. Poll taxes began to be instituted to keep many blacks from voting. White supremacy organizations intimidated those who wanted to vote.

State by state in the old Confederacy, blacks were losing their rights, and finally white supremacy was justified by the United States Supreme Court in 1896. In 1891, the Louisiana legislature ordered that trains within the state were to be segregated. The following year, Homer A. Plessy, a black man, bought a first-class ticket and took a seat in a white-only car. He was arrested and charged with violating the 1891 law. The case reached the Supreme Court. In a decision which allowed overt discrimination for well over half a century, the Court ruled that Plessy had not been denied his rights and set forth the "separate but equal" doctrine which came to apply to trams and trains, public education, colleges, drinking fountains, restaurants and lunch counters, theatres, and much else.⁵ Blacks were routinely called "nigger," "coon," "boy," and other derogatory words.

The South once again was a closed society and blacks were not slaves but they were not free. Discrimination fouled the lives of blacks and whites alike. This was the South known to Dr. Martin Luther King, Jr. and the other leaders of the black revolution which officially began with the Montgomery bus boycott, and of great significance, the huge numbers of African Americans who had lived their entire lives under this degrading system of segregation.

As an institution, the Klan had a short life, but the intimidation of blacks was pervasive in the south. To enforce "separate and equal" {actually "separate and unequal") throughout former slave states, white mobs lynched citizens, mostly black men. Law officials seldom interfered, and the lynchers were not brought to justice. This mob action, with widespread white support, was most often applied to blacks who were an economic threat, who disrespected or fought and struck a white man, or who raped a white woman or was accused of that rape, or who demanded rights given in the Fourteenth and Fifteenth Amendments. A reign of terror kept the South segregated.⁶

****

Gandhi as a student in London was treated well. He had no problems in finding lodging. He felt no discrimination in restaurants, trains, trolleys, libraries, theatres, or stores. A young attorney, he went to South Africa planning a one year stay. Once he arrived in Natal in 1893, he found he was regarded as, and called, "a coolie," in spite of his being member of a distinguished family and in spite of his legal studies in the Inner Temple in London.

Gandhi was quick to learn that Indians were needed for manual labor in the rich agricultural state of Natal, but these workers were abused and denied basic rights. Owners could expect sizeable financial returns by using cheap labor.

Introduction   xiii

A handbook for emigrants published in 1859 for the Colony of Natal promised that a prospective European settler with a capital of £500 could purchase 200 acres of land (£100) and meet all expenses of establishing a sugar plantation which in two years, at the first harvest of sugar cane, would bring a return of £800. The native laborers were to be paid 7 shillings a month. The total labor cost including "mealies," (maize porridge), would be £72 a year.[7] Of course, this prospectus left out problems of too little or too much rain, insect infestations, problems in finding laborers, and fluctuating prices for the harvested crop. Still, large profits could be made in Natal.

Unfortunately for the European owners of farms, most natives in Natal did not wish to take such employment. Without needed labor, the Natal government then requested the Indian government to allow indentured laborers to come for a five year period, and the request was granted. Indian laborers, largely Hindus, began to arrive in 1860.

During the Indenture period, Indians were virtual slaves. They had no choice of employer, were forced to live on the farms and were unable to leave without permission. They received 10 shillings a month. As it was necessary to supplement the meager diet provided by the owners and also buy clothes which were not provided, it was estimated that the average indentured servant possessed 6 pence a month after providing those necessities. The British government chose to allow this peonage.

Large numbers of indentured laborers chose to stay in Natal once they had served their indentures. Some moved to other colonies, and they found that the Boers in the Transvaal and the Orange Free State were even more intolerant than the English. Others worked in the mines.

Many of the Indians who stayed established small truck farms and quickly became the largest suppliers of fresh fruits and vegetables to the inhabitants, thereby becoming an economic threat to European truck farmers.

In addition, a considerable number of Indians, mostly Muslims, paid their own way and set up shop as merchants and traders. They, too, were successful, and Europeans saw them as an economic threat. Europeans in the colonies began to look for ways to harass Indians and force them to return to India. Naturally, they also wanted more Indians brought in for the labor force, but they would be allowed to stay only for the period of their indenture.[8]

****

For decades after the end of the Civil War, most black people in the South worked as cooks or maids or menial laborers for white people in towns and cities, or they stayed on farms as sharecroppers. The white owners of those farms provided a shack, mules, seeds, fertilizer, inadequate food, and the black sharecropper gave one half or more of the money for the crops to the landowner.[9] In South Africa and in the former Confederate states, the whites wanted people of color to remain in near peonage. The British government and the American government supported this exploitation of labor.

****

When Gandhi reached South Africa, Europeans who controlled the governments of the colonies had already begun to pass oppressive laws against Indians. Heavy taxes were proposed and then enacted. Segregation laws were similar to those in the South. Gandhi wrote this chilling passage about the words of extremist segregationists in South Africa: "We [Indians] are the 'Asian dirt' to be 'heartily cursed,' we are 'chokeful of vice' and 'we live upon rice,' we are 'stinking coolie' living on 'the smell of an oiled rag,' we are 'the black vermin,' we are described in the Statute books as 'semi-barbarous Asiatics, or persons belonging to the uncivilized races of Asia.' We 'breed like rabbits' and a gentleman at a meeting lately held in Durban said, he 'was sorry we could not be shot like them.'"[10]

****

Extremists in the South thought about blacks in similar ways. Even small black children were mistreated. When Martin Luther King, Jr. was about

Introduction

eight, he and his mother were in an Atlanta department store. Suddenly, he was slapped by a white woman who called out, "You are that nigger that stepped on my foot.'[11] There was nothing he could do about this injustice. The Kings lived comfortably; the elder King ministered to a large congregation. The elder Reverend King was still a nigger, as was his son.

****

Some South Africans were less vocal and less harsh than the extremists Gandhi wrote about, but most Europeans went along with the belief in white supremacy because they believed it or they did not wish to be singled out as non-believers in segregation. A few, a very few, Europeans disapproved of the denunciations and harassment of Indians. At the same time, a few, a very few, whites in the American South supported the rights of African Americans.

When Gandhi arrived in South Africa, he was an Anglo-Indian gentleman assuming and expecting all the privileges of the elite. He mistakenly believed that Indians were to receive all the rights of British subjects. Most Europeans in the South African colonies held racist views, and the government in London largely chose to let the colonies go their own way in racial matters. Over and over again, Gandhi found it difficult to travel first-class or to stay in up-scale hotels. He suffered indignity after indignity, all the time trying to believe in an idealized British Empire.

****

Martin Luther King, Jr., Rosa Parks, black physicians and teachers, maids, cooks, menial laborers had no illusions about segregation and the indignities showered upon them.

****

Racism affecting Indians in South Africa and affecting black people in the former Confederate states in the years 1893–1914 are similar. Racism finally forced Gandhi and thousands of others to protest nonviolently. The indignities of segregation were at the root of Rosa Parks refusing to give up her bus seat to a white man, and the resulting bus boycott brought about the emergence of Dr. King as nonviolent leader very similar to Gandhi in nonviolent methodology.

In this study, the emphasis is on Gandhi and racism and the parallels with racism in the United States.

Introduction   xvii

NOTES

1. David Gilmour, *The Ruling Caste*, p. 5; Joseph Lelyveld, *Great Soul*, p. 11,
2. Gilmour, *The Ruling Caste*, p. 1.
3. Constitution for the United States of America.
4. Darlene Clark Hine, William C. Hine, and Stanley Harrold, *The African-American Odyssey*, pp. 277–278.
5. Ibid., pp. 315–316.
6. Ibid., pp. 307–331.
7. Robert James Mann, editor, *The Colony of Natal: An Account of the Characteristics and Capabilities of this English Dependency. Published under the Authority of the Government, for the Guidance and Information of Emigrants*, pp. 80–83.
8. M. K. Gandhi, *Satyagraha in South Africa*, pp. 38–63.
9. Hine, Hine, and Harrold, *The African-American Odyssey*, p. 324.
10. M. K, Gandhi, *The Collected Works of Mahatma Gandhi*, II:4.
11. Martin Luther King, Jr., *The Autobiography of Martin Luther King, Jr.*, pp. 8–9.

Introduction

M. K. Gandhi's First Nonviolent Campaign

Chapter I

Before South Africa

Early Life in India

Mohandas Karamchand Gandhi was born on October 2, 1869, in Porbandar, India. The Gandhis were members of the *Bania* (commercial) caste, and Gandhi was born in the large three story home where the extended family lived. The Gandhis were prominent residents; Gandhi's grandfather and father were prime ministers of states ruled by Indian princes.[1]

Porbandar, a coastal state north of Bombay where the walls and buildings were of white stones, had a population of just under 18,000. In 1871, Gandhi's father was called to Rajkot, a larger city with a population of just under 25,000, which offered more educational advantages for the three Gandhi sons, Mohandas being the youngest.[2] Gandhi's father, called Kaba, lost his first two wives, but before their deaths, he had two daughters from these marriages. His third wife was an invalid, and there were no children. Because of her poor health, he was allowed to marry again. Kaba's fourth wife was the mother of one daughter and three sons.

Young Mohandas's father and grandfather were incorruptible and never accumulated wealth as many other high officials did. Both men were in difficult positions, for they had to please the prince and also the Agent, who represented the British government and overlooked the affairs of the state. The Prime Minister was often caught up in the quarrels between the prince and his court and the sometimes heavy hand of the British Raj, represented by the Agent.

Gandhi characterized his father as "truthful, brave and generous, but short-tempered."[3] His short temper may well have been caused by the difficulties he faced in placating the prince and the British Agent. Kaba Gandhi was loyal to the British Empire, which provided the underpinning of the hundreds of princely states. Gandhi's father was not a well-educated man; he spoke and read Gujarati, the language of the area, but did not know English. Much of Kaba's time was taken up with intrigue and scheming. The adult Mohandas rejected his father's brand of politics. Kaba had not received religious training, but he did visit temples and listened to religious talks.[4] During his last illness, he would quote passages from the *Bhagavad-Gita*.

In his *Autobiography*, Gandhi makes one curious statement about his father: "To a certain extent he might have been given to carnal pleasure. For he married for the fourth time when he was over forty."[5] The son gives no examples to support this speculation; he seems not to have noticed that no sons were born to his father's first three marriages and that Kaba Gandhi undoubtedly wished to have sons to carry on the family name.

Gandhi considered his mother to be a saint, and by implication he regarded his father as a sexual sinner. Gandhi's mother visited the Vaishnava temple daily and kept religious vows no matter the state of her health. She would limit herself to one meal a day; at other times, she would fast every other day. Once she vowed to refrain from food unless she saw the sun that day. During the rainy season, the children would rush inside to report the sun was out, but by the time she ventured outside, the sun would have disappeared. "That does not matter," she would say, "God did not want me to eat today."[6] She set an example for Gandhi's later fasts.

Before South Africa

Gandhi remembered his mother as a woman with common sense. The women in the courts of the princes, he reported, praised her intelligence. We can assume she also represented Kaba Gandhi's considered opinions when matters of state were discussed by the women.

When young Gandhi was about four his father was called to Rajkot, the family joining him after three years. Mohandas entered primary school. When he was twelve, he enrolled in Alfred High School, where the instruction in the later years was in English. This school was part of the educational mission of the British to bring the blessings of civilization to so-called backward regions and also to train future leaders. As T. B. Macaulay, the proponent of this new educational approach in India asserted, the new schools would teach "a class of persons, Indian in blood and colour, but English in taste, in opinion, in morals and in intellect."[7] For years, Gandhi attempted to live up to these standards.

The family had chosen Mohandas to be the one son to receive the best education, and he would be expected, at a later time, to help provide material comfort for the extended family. His parents held strong opinions, but Mohandas was capable of independent thought; he had misgivings about his mother's belief that untouchables should not be touched. He was not, though, in open revolt against Hindu beliefs, but he did experiment with smoking and eating meat.[8]

Young Gandhi followed the example of his father and was intent on telling the truth, even when it caused him problems. When he was in his early years in high school, Mr. Giles, the Educational Inspector, came for a visit. As part of an exercise, the students were to spell "kettle." Gandhi misspelled the word, and the teacher of the class, using the point of his shoe, prompted him to copy the correct spelling from a fellow-student's slate. Gandhi refused, and he was the only boy who could not spell "kettle." The teacher thought Gandhi acted stupidly, but Gandhi, early and late in life, was opposed to copying and plagiarism.[9]

Gandhi was a quiet, bright student in school, though he details his awkwardness, shyness, and lack of social and athletic skills in his *Autobiography*. His educational progress was slowed by his child marriage which took place when he was not quite thirteen. He lost almost a year in high school because of the elaborate ceremonials surrounding his marriage. His bride in this arranged marriage was Kasturba Makanji Kapadia, from a wealthy family in Porbandar. She was spirited, illiterate, and a few months older than the groom. Gandhi's father, at great expense, arranged the marriage of Mohandas, his brother Karsandas, and a cousin all in the same ceremonies, a saving of expenses. Writing in his *Autobiography*, Gandhi referred to child marriage preposterous.[10] Gandhi and his bride were temperamentally unsuited to one another, and the marriage was often troubled.

In 1882, marriage did not mean anything more to Mohandas "than the prospect of good clothes to wear, drum beating, marriage processions, rich dinners and a strange girl to play with. The carnal desire came later."[11]

Gandhi was coached on his behavior on the wedding night. He quickly became an autocratic husband, and Kasturba turned out not to be a meek wife. She was intent on going out when she pleased, seeing her own friends. She was unlettered and resisted his efforts to teach her.

Gandhi became a jealous child-husband. He had no reason to distrust Kasturba's faithfulness, but he did. He wrote about his jealousy in the chapter "Playing the Husband," a painful recreation of his confusion. He was clearly unready to be a husband.[12]

Gandhi wrote about suspicions of his wife in quite another context. In high school he met, through his older brother Karsandas, Sheikh Mehtab, a Muslim son of a jailor, who lived across the street from the Gandhis. Mehtab was athletic, fearless, outgoing, and with advanced ideas not acceptable to the elder Gandhis. (In the *Autobiography*, Gandhi never gives Mehtab's name; he is identified as a friend.) Mehtab was everything Gandhi was not, and he seemed determined to capture the friendship of the shy young man whose father held high positions. Gandhi had one other friend in school, but Mehtab somehow managed to interfere with this friendship, leaving Mehtab as Gandhi's sole intimate friend. At first, Mehtab seems to have appealed to the small Gandhi because he protected him from school bullies.

Mehtab set about liberating Gandhi from his conventional beliefs, including the vegetarian diet followed by Gandhi's family. Mehtab, a Muslim, did not observe the Hindu injunctions against eating meat. Mehtab enforced the meaning of the doggerel verse in Gujarati then popular with schoolboys:

> Behold the mighty Englishman
>
> He rules the Indian small,
>
> Because being a meat-eater,
>
> He is five cubits tall.[13]

Implicit in this verse is opposition to British rule of India. Without fully understanding the political message of the verse, Gandhi was acting in opposition to his father, who was intimately involved with the British Raj, even though he found himself at times at odds with the British agents overseeing the princedoms.

Mehtab convinced Gandhi that there were ample reasons for him to eat meat, and he prepared meat meals for him and took him to a restaurant where meat was served as a main dish. He told Gandhi that meat-eating would make him "strong and daring, and that, if the whole country took to meat-eating, the English would be overcome."[14]

For about a year, Gandhi became a dietary rebel, but he had to hide his meat-eating from his parents. Mehtab lost that particular battle, for Gandhi decided that he could not lie to his parents. He returned to a vegetarian diet, and his parents did not know about his apostasy.

Gandhi came to rationalize that he would reform his "bad boy" friend, but he had no more success in that venture than Lady Byron had in changing the ways of her wayward husband. Gandhi went on believing the best about his friend, and for many years his eyes were closed to Mehtab's behavior.[15]

Mehtab was a student at Alfred High School, although some years ahead of Gandhi. One wonders if Mehtab did not read Shakespeare's *Othello* and adapt some of Iago's schemes against Desdemona to make Othello jealous. Mehtab fanned Gandhi's suspicions about Kasturba, suspicions which were not spelled out in the *Autobiography* but were undoubtedly sexual. Gandhi could not bring himself, even in his text which was devoted to telling the truth, to divulge just what suspicions he had about his wife. Instead, he wrote, "I have never forgiven myself the violence of which I have been guilty in often having pained my wife by acting on this information."[16]

In this incident with Kasturba, Mehtab, and himself, Gandhi draws the curtain over much of the truth. In the concluding paragraph on his chapter on "Tragedy" in his *Autobiography*, he wrote: "The canker of suspicion was rooted out only when I understood *Ahimsa* in all its bearings. I saw then the glory of *Brahmacharya* and realized that the wife is not the husband's bondslave, but his companion and his helpmate, and an equal partner in all his joys and sorrows—as free as the husband to choose her own path."[17] (In his footnote on this passage, Gandhi defines *ahimsa* as "literally not-hurting, non-violence" and *brahmacharya* as "literally conduct that leads one to God. Its technical meaning is self-restraint, particularly mastery over the sexual organ.")

Gandhi left several things unresolved. He does not indicate how the immediate conflict was resolved. He does not explain his blind devotion to Mehtab, particularly relevant since the friendship did not end. Additionally, Gandhi is vague about just when he realized—and acted upon—his newfound-knowledge that a wife was an equal partner. In fact, he was extremely slow to change his views about the rights of women. Conflicts with his wife continued through the South Africa years.

Speculating about the relationship between Gandhi and Mehtab, Erik Erikson in *Gandhi's Truth* did not believe that it was a "passing experiment with homosexuality..." Mehtab was alive when Gandhi wrote his *Autobiography*, and there were obvious restraints on what he could reveal. Erikson does observe, "...Any intense friendship among men which excludes and demeans women cannot be without a homosexual element." On the question of "possible experiment with homosexuality," Erikson gives two answers without convincing proof for either: No and Perhaps.[18] There does appear to be a homoerotic element in the relationship, however.

Apparently following the episode of Gandhi's suspicions about his wife's unfaithfulness, Mehtab convinced him to go to a prostitute. It is possible that a distressed Kasturba may have been unwilling to have sex with her jealous husband, or she may have returned to her family, leaving her husband with no sexual outlets. Mehtab may well have made Gandhi feel unsure about his sexual prowess; if that is so, Mehtab may have argued that if Kasturba were told that her husband was going to prostitutes, she would be more willing to accede to his sexual demands.

Mehtab, three or four years older than Gandhi, and more sexually mature, may have held the view that faithfulness to a wife was hopelessly out-of-date, and that men should be free to follow their sexual desires. Whatever the reasons for the trip to the bordello, Mehtab took Gandhi to a brothel, gave instructions, indicating Mehtab was well-acquainted with prostitutes, and the bill was paid. Once Gandhi was in the room with the woman he was "almost struck blind and dumb." As he sat on the bed with her, he was unable to speak. She showed him to the door "with abuses and insults."[19] In his *Autobiography*, Gandhi gave a moralistic evaluation of this event, saying God had saved him: Man, he wrote, often succumbed to temptation even though he resisted it, but "Providence often intercedes and saves him in spite of himself."[20]

Gandhi wrote in his *Autobiography* about another of his transgressions, again, one suspects, with Mehtab at the center. Gandhi's older brother Karsandas fell into debt because of his meat-eating experiments. Mehtab fostered the revolt of Mohandas and Karsandas against the vegetarianism of Hinduism. Karsandas needed 25 rupees to clear his debt. Mohandas, then fifteen, was convinced to break off a piece of Karsandas's gold armlet, and the gold was sold. It isn't clear why Karsandas did not do his own thieving. Perhaps Mehtab was testing to see how far Mohandas could be led astray.[21]

In his *Autobiography*, Gandhi does not admit that Mehtab was involved in planning this incident with the gold armlet. Gandhi is perhaps protecting himself from admitting that he was continuing a relationship with an untrustworthy friend. What is clear is that Gandhi felt guilty about the theft and wanted to confess to his ill father. He could not bring himself to speak directly but instead wrote out his confession, asked to be punished, and requested his father "not to punish himself for my offence. I also pledged myself never to steal in future."[22]

Lying on his sick-bed, the elder Gandhi read the note, cried, and then tore up the confession. Gandhi wrote that his father's tears "Washed my sin away."[23] Gandhi the moralist then gave this later interpretation: the incident was more than a father's love, but was pure *Ahimsa* (nonviolence).

Gandhi's mother, brother Laxmidas, and Kasturba all recognized what a bad influence Mehtab was on Mohandas. They did not press their objections strenuously, for Mohandas was a favored son. What objections they did express were rejected by Mohandas who continued to believe he could reform his friend. It is true that Mohandas was amused by Mehtab and shared some of his wayward friend's progressive views.[24] Kasturba seems to have known that Mehtab was her enemy.

During his father's illness, Mohandas spent much time nursing him. Part of the elder Gandhi's physical problems came from an injury sustained on his trip from Rajkot to Porbandar to participate in the marriage of his two sons and his nephew. Young Gandhi prepared drugs for his father, gave him his medicine, and massaged his legs before studying for his high school courses. He also had obligations as a child-husband, with his wife Kasturba pregnant with their first child.

While Gandhi massaged his father's legs, his thoughts were on the bedroom he shared with his child-bride. When he wrote his *Autobiography*, he had long since become chaste as part of his self-purification, but in the scenes describing his father's death, he dwells on his shame for what he considered his youthful lustfulness.[25]

Gandhi was massaging his father's legs at about 10:30 or 11 p.m., when his uncle, sitting with Kaba Gandhi, offered to relieve his nephew. Young Gandhi returned to the room he shared with his wife, woke her, and, the text infers, began sex. Five minutes or so later, a servant arrived to report that Kaba Gandhi was "very ill," but the truth was that he was dead. Gandhi was "deeply ashamed and miserable."[26] He was distressed that he was not with his father at the time of death. He was even more overcome with remorse because he was having sex with his pregnant wife during the elder Gandhi's dying moments. This one incident scarred Gandhi's views on sexual matters, as seen later in some of his actions in South Africa. The first baby lived only a few days, but their second child, a son Harilal, was born in the spring of 1888, not long before Gandhi departed for London.

During his high school days, when he was also nursing his father, he was often present when Muslim and Farsi friends discussed religion with the elder Gandhi. The son began to develop a tolerance for most religious faiths, but at that time he disliked Christianity. Christian missionaries standing near the high school would be "pouring abuse on Hindus and their gods."[27] Gandhi was disturbed by stories that Christian converts ate meat, drank liquor, and wore European clothes.

Mohandas had little specific knowledge about world religions, but his mother was deeply religious and his father also quoted passages from the *Bhagavad-Gita* during his illness. Mohandas was just beginning to contemplate ideas on morality, but just how long this activity went on is not known. Certainly it was a mere glimmer during his high school days, but his later, mature belief was "that morality is the basis of things, and that truth is the substance of all morality."[28]

In 1887 Gandhi passed his examinations and left high school. He wanted to attend college in Bombay, but family finances could not afford those costs. Instead, he entered Samaldas College in Bhavnagar, where his one term there was a failure. His English was imperfect, he could not follow the lectures, and in fact he was not interested in them. Gandhi may have, at least unconsciously, deliberately failed his term at college, for he had by then developed a strong desire to study in London. His father had spoken of the advantages of education in England. A family friend believed that with proper education Gandhi could also be a Prime Minister —or more.

Gandhi was interested in studying medicine, but the necessity to dissect dead bodies caused relatives to object to that course of study. It was decided that law would be a better choice for him. There were prolonged talks about his future, but Kasturba does not seem to have been involved in these discussions, nor to have played a role in the planning of their future life. Gandhi's mother, though, was deeply involved. She had many—and continuing—objections to her son's travelling to England for a long period of time, but he finally overcame his mother's worries when he swore to refrain from meat, liquor, and sex during his study abroad.[29]

Raising the necessary funds was a major problem for the family, and his elder brother Laxmidas was put in charge of that task. The final cost was more than the first estimate; the three years spent in London cost 13,000 rupees. Mohandas assisted his brother by approaching Frederick Lely, the British-appointed administrator of Porbandar, for state help with expenses. The Gandhi family was known to Lely because two generations of Gandhis had served as Prime Minister in that area. Gandhi had memorized his sentences that he was to say to Mr. Lely, but upon admission to the presence of this august man, he found Lely in a hurry. Lely commented that the state was poor and then said to Gandhi curtly: "Pass your B.A. first and then see me. No help can be given now." Lely then hurried up the steps.[30] Gandhi had bowed low and had saluted Lely with both hands, but he was brusquely dismissed. Gandhi was to learn in South Africa and India that many British and European administrators were racially insensitive. The Raj did not consider Indians to be full citizens of the Empire.

****

Gandhi was treated with disdain by Lely, but slaves in the United States were treated worse. Josiah Henson, whose life story was used by Harriet Beecher Stowe in creating the character of Uncle Tom, was a slave on the Maryland farm of Isaac Riley. When Henson was nineteen or twenty years old, one of his week-end jobs was to accompany his dissipated master to the local cock fights and horse races, meetings fueled by cheap liquor, and brawls often broke out. Henson and other slaves attending their masters had to rush into the melee to rescue their owners. At one of the donnybrooks, Riley was quarreling with Brute Litton, overseer for Riley's brother. During the fight, Litton was injured and blamed Henson. A week later, Litton took his revenge. With the help of three slaves, Litton accosted Henson, who was terribly beaten; he sustained a broken arm and both shoulder blades were also broken. At length, Litton's vengeance was satisfied, he stopped the beating, and told Henson "to learn what it was to strike a white man."

In great pain, Henson returned to Riley, who refused to call a physician for the slave because, as he said, "A nigger will get well anyway." Riley's sister bound his wounds as best she could, but he was never again able to raise his arms over his head.[31]

****

Lely was a powerful figure in the Raj, fully aware of his power over the man of color, Gandhi. Lely did not use physical force against Gandhi but his words and arrogance scarred the young Indian who supported Queen Victoria and the Empire.

The process of getting his mother's approval and the raising of funds was long and psychologically taxing. During this trying time, Gandhi quarreled with Mehtab, but the nature of the disagreement is not known. On a city street, thinking about the problem with his friend, Gandhi hit his head on a carriage and afterwards fainted.

Mehtab the trickster and sometime villain involved himself in fund raising for Mohandas. A relative of the Gandhis had indicated that he was willing to provide some funds for Mohandas to study abroad, but Gandhi's mother was astute and believed that no money would be forthcoming. Mehtab forged a letter, using Gandhi's name, reminding the relative of his promise and requesting 5,000 rupees. The request failed, as Mrs. Gandhi knew it would, and she was amused. Mohandas enjoyed his friend's audacity. Mehtab was, at least temporarily, in the good graces of Gandhi's mother.[32]

Laxmidas considered many suggestions as he sought funds. Should Kasturba's jewelry be sold? Yes, it was. Should other relatives be approached? Yes. Finally the funds were found, and Gandhi, Laxmidas, Mehtab, and one other friend went to Bombay where Gandhi's ship would depart. There they were to discover that the next sailing was several weeks away. Laxmidas left the funds Mohandas needed with Kasturbta's brother, who lived in Bombay, and returned home. Mohandas and his friends remained, but there were new problems. As the days went by, Gandhi's caste became more opposed to his leaving India and called him to appear before it.

The Head of the caste was a distant relative and had been on friendly terms with Gandhi's father. He said: "In the opinion of the caste, your proposal to go to England is not proper. Our religion forbids voyages abroad. We have also heard that it is not possible to live there without compromising our religion. One is obliged to eat and drink with Europeans!"

Gandhi responded: "I do not think it is at all against our religion to go to England. I intend going there for further studies. And I have already solemnly promised to my mother to abstain from three things you fear most. I am sure the vows will keep me safe."

"But we tell you that it is not possible to keep our religion there. You know my relations with your father and you ought to listen to my advice."

"I know those relations. And you are as an elder to me. But I am helpless in this matter. I cannot alter my resolve to go to England. My father's friend and adviser, who is a learned Brahman, sees no objection to my going to England, and my mother and brother have also given me their permission."

"But will you disregard the orders of the caste?"

"I am really helpless. I think the caste should not interfere in the matter."

The head of the caste was incensed, swore at Gandhi, and made his pronouncement: "This boy shall be treated as an outcaste from today. Whoever helps him or goes to see him off at the dock shall be punishable with a fine of one rupee four annas."[33]

Being cast from the caste did not deter Gandhi; he had learned, most probably from Mehtab, to view the Hindu caste system with disdain. He worried that Laxmidas would be concerned, but Laxmidas was not. This kind of steely resolve stayed with Gandhi the rest of his life.

Mohandas's infatuation with Mehtab did not diminish, and the two corresponded after Gandhi arrived in London. Without doubt, Mehtab carried information from the letters he received from Mohandas to the Gandhis in Rajkot, but given his prior history he probably spread misinformation also.[34]

The problems of departure were still not over. Kasturba's brother refused to hand over the funds entrusted to him because of the ruling of the caste making Gandhi an outcaste. Gandhi overcame his natural shyness and borrowed the necessary money from a friend of the family.[35]

Ambition was driving Gandhi; he wrote: "...[if] I go to England, not only shall I become a barrister...but I shall be able to see England, the land of philosophers and poets, the centre of civilization."[36]

Wearing newly-purchased European-style clothes, Gandhi left Bombay on September 4, 1888, on the *Clyde*.

Notes

1. For biographical information, we have used Gandhi, *Autobiography: My Experiments with Truth*, subsequently referred to as *Autobiography*; Rajmohan Gandhi, *Mohandas: A True Story of a Man, His People, and an Empire*, subsequently referred to as *Mohandas*; and Pyarelal, *The Early Phase*.
2. Rajmohan Gandhi, *Mohandas*, p. 4; James D. Hunt, *Gandhi in London*, p. 3.
3. Gandhi, *Autobiography*, p. 12.
4. Ibid., p. 12; Gandhi, *Collected Works*, 24:170.
5. Gandhi, *Autobiography*, p. 12.
6. Ibid., p. 13.
7. Quoted in Hunt, *Gandhi in London*, p. 4.
8. Rajmohan Gandhi, *Mohandas*, p. 5.
9. Gandhi, *Autobiography*, 15–16.
10. Ibid., p. 18.
11. Ibid., p. 19.
12. Ibid., p. 22–25.
13. Ibid., p. 33.
14. Ibid., p. 33; Rajmohan Gandhi, *Mohandas*, pp. 8–10.
15. Gandhi, *Autobiography*, pp. 31, 38.
16. Ibid., p. 38.
17. Ibid., p. 38.
18. Erik Erikson, *Gandhi's Truth*, p. 135. Erikson thinks that there was no homosexual activity because Gandhi was writing a truthful account and would have written about it had it happened.
19. Gandhi, *Autobiography*, p. 37.
20. Ibid., p. 37.
21. Ibid., pp. 40–41; Rajmohan Gandhi, *Mohandas*, p. 11.
22. Gandhi, *Autobiography*, p. 41.
23. Ibid., p. 41.
24. Rajmohan Gandhi, *Mohandas*, p. 16.
25. Gandhi, *Autobiography*, pp. 45–46.
26. Ibid., p. 45.
27. Ibid., 49.
28. Ibid., p. 50–51.

29. Ibid., p. 56.
30. Ibid., p. 55.
31. Josiah Henson, *Father Henson's Story of His Own Life*, pp. 33–39.
32. Rajmohan Gandhi, *Mohandas*, p. 21.
33. Gandhi, *Autobiography*, pp. 57–58.
34. Erik Erickson in *Gandhi's Truth* wrote: "Mehtab was among those who saw him off in Bombay. Being literate, he was to receive and deliver all the letters Mohandas would write his stubbornly illiterate wife; what an arrangement for endless, fateful mischief!" (pp. 139–40). Erikson does not give a reference for the statement that Mehtab carried Gandhi's letters to Kasturba. It is more likely that those letters were sent through Laxmidas, who was literate. Still, it is probable that Mehtab caused mischief in the Gandhi family in Rajkot while Gandhi was studying in London. Erikson made other statements about Gandhi and Mehtab in *Gandhi's Truth*: "Mehtab's role in [Mohandas's] life was obviously one of elemental significance, not only because the young Muslim was such a 'devil,' but because Mohandas chose him and stubbornly held onto him in order to test, I believe, the devil in himself." (p. 135). "...Mehtab played perfectly the personage on whom to project one's personal devil and thus became the personification of Mohandas' negative identity, that is, of everything in himself which he tried to isolate and subdue and which yet was part of him." (p. 135).
35. Pyarelal, *The Early Years*, p. 224.
36. Ibid., p. 224.

Chapter II

Before South Africa

Student Years in London

Gandhi shared a cabin on the *Clyde* with Tryambakrai Mazmudar, a *vakil* or pleader, from the princely state of Junagadh. Mazmudar was a mature man planning to study to be a barrister in order to burnish his law credentials.[1] He was outgoing and moved easily among the English-speaking passengers. Gandhi was shy and kept to the cabin; he had trouble speaking and understanding English; he did not know how to use knives and forks. Afraid that food in the dining room was not truly vegetarian, he ate the fruits and sweets he had brought with him.

One time when Gandhi ventured out of his cabin, an older man initiated a conversation, assuring the young Hindu he could not survive in England without eating meat. Gandhi was obstinate; he had made a promise to his mother and would not break it. If it were necessary to eat meat 1n London, he would return to India.[2]

When the *Clyde* stopped in Brindisi on the Adriatic Sea, a tout offered a beautiful fourteen year old girl to Gandhi. Gandhi declined and ordered the tout away. Within a short period of time he kept two of his vows: not to eat meat and to refrain from sexual activities.[3]

The *Clyde* arrived in Tilbury on September 29, 1888. Gandhi had been wearing a black suit on the ship, but he debarked in white flannels, the only male passenger so dressed. The shy Gandhi had made a sartorial blunder his first day in England. Thus attired, he took a train into London and checked into the expensive Victoria Hotel.[4]

On the evening of his arrival, he was met by Dr. P. J. Mehta, a graduate of Bombay's Grant Medical College, who was studying advanced medicine and law in London. Dr. Mehta was amused by Gandhi's inappropriate attire. Gandhi was guilty of another faux pas as he was speaking with Dr. Mehta. He picked up the doctor's top hat and ran his hand over it the wrong way, disturbing the fur. Dr. Mehta reacted angrily and stopped the innocent abroad. He then gave Gandhi a lesson in European etiquette:

"Do not touch other people's things."

"Do not ask questions as we usually do in India on first acquaintance."

"Do not talk loudly."

"[N]ever address people as 'sir' whilst speaking to them as we do in India; only servants and subordinates address their masters that way."[5]

Dr. Mehta rightly saw that Gandhi needed to live with an English family to learn the rules of society and to perfect his English. At first, Gandhi moved out of the hotel to cheap rooms and then to an English home in Richmond, where fellow Indian Dalpatram Shukla already lived. Shukla was studying to be a barrister and could help explain English ways to Gandhi. The first weeks were extremely difficult for Gandhi who was homesick and confused by the strange society he now inhabited.

Shukla's educational goals were the same as Gandhi's, but the two did not become close personal friends, though Shukla did introduce Gandhi to the reading of newspapers. Shukla read three: the conservative *Daily*

Telegraph, the liberal *Daily News* and the combative *Pall Mall Gazette*, edited by W. T. Stead. In this journal, Stead was the defender of the downtrodden. Among other topics, he dealt with child prostitution.[6] Gandhi began spending an hour reading these same papers, and during his stay in London he continued to read them. His reading helped improve his English and provided him with samples of clear, precise writing. It also exposed him to a variety of social and political ideas, as well as stories about civil and criminal matters.

It was not easy for Gandhi to travel from Richmond into London, and with the help of Shukla and Dr. Mehta he found a room in West Kensington in the home of a widow with two daughters. His landlady provided him with vegetarian meals, but the food was scanty and inadequate; he was always hungry. He was too shy to ask for more food, though the daughters of the house would sometimes give him an extra slice or two of bread.[7]

Gandhi wandered around looking for a vegetarian restaurant, and in November or December of 1888 he came upon the Central on Farrington Street. "The sight of it," Gandhi wrote, "filled me with the same joy that a child feels on getting a thing after its own heart." In the window of the Central he saw a copy of Henry Salt's *A Plea for Vegetarianism* (1886). He bought a copy for a shilling as he entered the restaurant. He had his first hearty meal since his arrival in England. He read Salt's book "from cover to cover and was very much impressed with it. From the date of reading this book, I may claim to have become a vegetarian by choice."[8]

Henry Salt was born to privilege in 1851 in India, the son of Colonel T. H. Salt of the Royal Bengal Artillery. His mother returned to England with Henry when he was young. He attended Eton and Cambridge with great success and returned to Eton as a master.

Salt remained at Eton until 1884, but he had come to view the world quite differently from his colleagues. He became a convert to vegetarianism and believed that Eton masters "were but cannibals in cap and gown." He was a socialist and an early member of the Fabian Society.

He and his wife were followers of Thoreau and lived a simple life. He was a biographer of skill and wrote a perceptive study of Thoreau. He worked for such causes as dietary reform, anti-vivisection, and animals' rights. In 1891 he founded the Humanitarian League which was devoted to "placing on record...a systematic and insistent protest against the numerous barbarisms of civilization—the cruelties inflicted by men on men, in the name of law, and the traditional habit and still more atrocious ill-treatment of the so-called lower animals, for the purpose of sport, 'science,' 'fashion,' and the gratification of an appetite for unnatural food."[9]

It was partially through Salt that Gandhi met other vegetarians and reformers. Both were members of the London Vegetarian Society and both attended the Vegetarian Federal Union in May of 1891. The two undoubtedly met at other times. Salt was part of a group of English reformers, including Edward Carpenter, that influenced Gandhi's world view.[10] In the vegetarian and reform circles he heard mention of Thoreau, Tolstoy, and many others. The English press, which Gandhi read daily, had articles about Tolstoy, Ruskin, Marx, and other unconventional writers and philosophers.

Gandhi's immediate need was to begin his study to become a barrister. He joined the Inner Temple, the most expensive and most prestigious of the four Inns of Court. James D. Hunt in his excellent *Gandhi in London* has a succinct discussion of the differences between solicitors and barristers: "The solicitors, who outnumber the barristers by a ratio of 10 to 1, appear in the lower courts and may be approached directly by clients for legal advice. Their training is long and arduous, and takes place in the law offices where they labor as 'articled clerks' under an apprenticeship system....The higher class of lawyers, or barristers, who have exclusive right of audience in all the superior courts, may not deal directly with clients but are engaged by solicitors when their special services are required."[11]

The formal requirements for the bar examinations were "serious but not severe." Students were to "keep" twelve terms, four terms a year, attend at least six dinners each term, and pass two examinations which were written and oral, one in Roman Law and the other in Common Law. Gandhi was a welcome guest at the dinners because wine was provided. Since he didn't drink, others at that table were even better wined.[12]

There were some lectures and textbooks for examinations. Gandhi bought the required texts for £10, and he read all of them. Tutorials were available, but Gandhi believed in "self-preparation" and avoided them. James D. Hunt in *Gandhi in London* lists the authors and titles of the texts Gandhi needed to master. Several of the texts were long and difficult, but Gandhi was especially interested in Joshua Williams's *Principles of the Law of Real Property*, which, he wrote, "read like a novel." He went through texts slowly; the *Common Law of England* took him nine months to master.[13]

For the Roman Law examination, a student had a choice; he could read a summary or the entire text of the Justinian Code. Gandhi chose to read the entire text in Latin. He had not studied Latin in high school, but he studied it in London and passed the Latin exam. Gandhi was a quick study, but his reading of the Latin text would have been helped by the English translation included in Thomas Collett Sandar's *The Institutes of Justinian* (1859). Gandhi took his Roman Law examination on March 25–28, 1890, passing 6th among 46 takers.[14]

Gandhi studied the textbooks carefully, often in the Inner Temple Library, allowing him to reduce the heating costs in his room. He took the Bar Finals on December 15–20, 1890 and learned on January 12, 1891, that he had passed, placing 34th out of 109 takers. He had no other obligations except to "keep" three more terms, which he did before returning to India.[15]

While he was reading the required texts and studying for his examinations, Gandhi was learning to adapt to English society. When he was living with an English family, he ate the bland food but looked forward to more vegetarian fare. Then, as a way of saving money and living a simpler life, he took rooms and cooked for himself. He prepared two meals a day. For breakfast he had porridge, stewed fruit and bread and butter. For supper he had bread and milk; and stewed fruit, or radishes. He had lunch at an inexpensive vegetarian restaurant. His studies abroad were costly, and he needed to save money, but he was also following the accounts of the virtues of simple life being proposed by Henry Salt and others whom Gandhi admired.[16]

Gandhi also lowered his living costs by walking wherever he needed to go in London, often several miles each day, another recommendation from the devotees of a simple life.[17]

In dress, however, Gandhi made a concerted effort to mimic an English gentleman. Students studying to become barristers were expected to maintain suitable dress. The English-style clothes he purchased in Bombay (probably chosen by Mehtab) were put aside. His new costume consisted of a high silk top hat, a rainbow-colored tie over a finely made cambric shirt, a morning coat over a vest, striped trousers, patent leather shoes and spats, leather gloves and a silver-headed cane.[18] Gandhi continued to dress fashionably once he returned to India and during many of his years in South Africa. He did, however, modify and simplify the extremes of his sartorial splendor in London.

Gandhi began what he was later to consider "the all too impossible task of becoming an English gentleman." He paid careful attention to the arranging of his tie, and he forced his unruly hair in place. He was told he needed to take lessons in dancing, French, and elocution, and to play the violin.

Gandhi paid £3 for a term of dancing instruction. After six lessons in three weeks, he found that he could not "achieve anything like rhythmic motion." Those classes stopped. The French lessons apparently were also short-lived. He did find a teacher of elocution and paid a fee of one guinea.

Before South Africa

He bought the text, Bell's *Standard Elocutionist*, but after two or three lessons he decided that since he was not going to remain in England, there was no reason to learn elocution. His reasoning was not sound; a barrister needed to speak clearly, and later, in South Africa and India, he gave many speeches. As Gandhi was extremely shy during his childhood and his years in London, elocution lessons would have helped him. He also did not learn to play the violin. Gandhi in his *Autobiography* wrote that the infatuation with becoming a gentleman lasted about three months: "The punctiliousness in dress persisted for years. But henceforth I became a student."[19]

Early in his years in London, Gandhi developed interests in religion. To learn about English religion, he began attending protestant churches on a regular basis, most often the City Temple Congregational Church.[20] He seemed to have no interest in the Church of England or the Catholic Church. He soon met Bertram and Archibald Keightley, wealthy uncle and nephew (not brothers, as Gandhi recalled in his *Autobiography*) who were Theosophists, a society founded by Helena Blavatsky in 1875. Theosophy was indebted to Hindu and Buddhist thought and urged members to read Hindu religious texts. There was a strong element of the occult in the society, but Gandhi especially rejected that part of Theosophy.[21]

The Keightleys had been reading Sir Edwin Arnold's translation of the *Bhagavad-Gita*, which he titled *The Song Celestial*. Gandhi had to admit that he had not read the Hindu religious text in Sanskrit or in Gujarati. His Sanskrit was, he wrote, "meagre, still I hoped to be able to understand the original to the extent of telling where the translation failed to bring out the meaning."[22] As he read Arnold's translation, he thought it the best, for it was faithful to the original text and did not read like a translation.

The *Gita*, as it is often called, contains the dialog between Krishna, God incarnate, and Arjuna, the great warrior who wants to stop the fighting in a fratricidal battle bringing tragedy to participants and families. Krishna advises him to do his duty and put aside all objections and continue the battle, for souls have no beginning or ending and therefore there is no death in battle. Arjuna is to do his duty as he takes Action, but he must renounce the fruits of Action. Verse 2 of Chapter 5 of the *Gita* sets forth an important concept in this religious text: "Renunciation and performance of action both lead to salvation; but of the two, *karmayoga* (performance) is better than *sannyasa* (renunciation)" (Gandhi's translation). Gandhi chose performance, but it should be done selflessly.[23]

Gandhi in his own translation of the *Gospel of Selfless Action or the Gita According to Gandhi* (1946) wrote that as early as 1888–1889 he felt the *Gita* "was not an historical work, but that, under the guise of physical warfare, it described the duel that perpetually went on in the hearts of mankind."[24] Most scholars, however, have rejected Gandhi's interpretation. Gandhi had turned against a literal reading of the text for an allegorical one.

The Keightleys also introduced Gandhi to Sir Edwin Arnold's account of Buddha entitled *The Light of Asia* (1879). Traditional Christians objected to Sir Edwin's tolerant attitude toward non-Christian religions, but Gandhi approved this approach and read the text with great interest.[25]

Theosophists stressed universal brotherhood and urged followers to read sacred texts and also Mme. Blavatsky's *Key to Philosophy*, which stimulated Gandhi to read more about Hinduism and, as he wrote, "disabused me of the notion fostered by the missionaries that Hinduism was rife with superstition."[26]

The Keightleys took Gandhi in 1889 to meet Mme. Blavatsky and Mrs. Annie Besant, formerly the wife of a minister, then an atheist, a socialist, and a proponent of birth control. She had only recently been converted to Theosophy. Gandhi went to Queen's Hall in August or September, 1889, to hear Mrs. Besant speak on "Why I Became a Theosophist," a masterful presentation of the philosophy of the society. She ended her speech, as Gandhi recalled it, by remarking "that she would be quite satisfied to have the epitaph written on her tomb that she had lived for truth and she died for truth."[27] Gandhi adapted that epitaph in part for the subtitle of his *Autobiography: The Story of My Experiments with Truth*.

Before South Africa

Gandhi remembered that he declined to join the Theosophical Society, but he seems to have taken out a six month associate membership on March 26, 1891, not long before he left London for India. He continued to read about other faiths, also; he read Carlyle's *Hero and Hero Worship* for its account of the Prophet Mohammed.

At a vegetarian boarding house Gandhi met a Christian man who did not eat meat nor drink alcohol. Gandhi told him about the Christian missionaries in Rajkot who reviled Hinduism. These missionaries were usually racists and religious bigots. The man urged Gandhi to read the Bible; there was some self-interest in that recommendation, for Gandhi slyly remarked that the man seemed to have been a Bible salesman. Gandhi purchased the deluxe version of the Bible with maps, concordances, and aids for the reader. He read Genesis, but the books that followed put him to sleep. He forced himself to read those books, but he had no interest in them and no understanding.[28]

In high school, under Mehtab's influence, Gandhi had wanted to free India from the British Raj, but in London he was making himself into an Anglo-Indian gentleman, and he quite naturally supported the Empire as it then existed. Otherwise, he would have taken special interest in the story of Moses who delivered his people from bondage.

The New Testament appealed to Gandhi, most especially the Sermon on the Mount (Luke: 6, 20-49 and Matthew 5: 3-48; 6: 1-34; 7: 1-29). He wrote specifically about the impact of the Sermon: "I compared it with the *Gita*. The verses, 'But I say unto you, that ye resist not evil; but whosoever shall smite thee on thy right cheek, turn to him the other also. And if any man take away thy coat let him have thy cloke too,' delighted me beyond measure. My young mind tried to unify the teaching of the *Gita*, the *Light of Asia*, and the Sermon on the Mount." He came to believe that renunciation of the fruits of Action—that is, selfless Action—was the highest form of religion.[29]

Did Gandhi recognize Mehtab's influence on him in these words from Luke 6:45: "...an evil man out of the evil treasure of his heart bringeth forth that which is evil"? Gandhi had deplored his devotion to a friend who spread rumors about Kasturba but the friendship continued. Mehtab saw Gandhi off to London, and was in contact during Gandhi's years in London, even borrowing money from him at a time when the Gandhi family finances were stretched thin to support him in his law studies.[30] Mehtab was a devious associate, but Gandhi was reluctant to disassociate himself from his friend.

Gandhi attended the funeral services for Charles Bradlaugh on January 30, 1891. Bradlaugh was known as a leading supporter of atheism in England. Annie Besant worked closely with him for many years before she defected to the Theosophical Society. He held many "advanced" ideas, including birth-control. When he was a member of Parliament, he was known as "the member for India" because of his advocacy for Indian rights.[31] Gandhi thought that every Indian in London attended the funeral, mostly because of Bradlaugh's support for the rights of Indians, not necessarily because of his views on atheism and birth control.

Gandhi had toyed with atheism when he was in high school; he did not have "any living faith in God."[32] Mehtab may well have encouraged him, but Gandhi's religious studies in London largely disabused him of his flirtation with atheism.

During his last months in London, after he had passed the bar examinations and had only to attend a few more dinners, Gandhi paid much more attention to vegetarianism and diet reform. He had met Josiah Oldfield, a Cambridge graduate in theology, who also was to become a barrister and a physician. Oldfield was editor of *The Vegetarian* and asked Gandhi to contribute articles to that publication. Gandhi agreed, and his articles show that he had mastered English: he wrote clearly and persuasively. He was, though, still shy when speaking at meetings. During his last three months in London, Gandhi and Oldfield took rooms together. Unlike Mehtab, Oldfield had a good influence on Gandhi, urging him to have a public life.

Gandhi wrote nine articles for the vegetarian journal between February and April, 1891.[33]

Gandhi was involved in a conflict between Arnold F. Hills, a wealthy industrialist who gave the Vegetarian movement much needed financial support, and Dr. Thomas R. Allinson, health crusader and social reformer. In his *A Book for Married Women*, Dr. Allinson advocated birth control. Mr. Hills thought Dr. Allinson's views were "immoral" and late in February 1891 asked the London Vegetarian Society to expel Dr. Allinson. Gandhi was opposed to birth control but thought Dr. Allinson had the right to his opinions. He prepared a speech supporting Dr. Allinson but was too shy to read it, and someone else did so. Mr. Hills carried the day, but Gandhi wrote, "Thus in the very first battle of the kind I found myself siding with the losing party. But I had comfort in the thought that the cause was right."[34]

Just before he was to depart for India, Gandhi attended a vegetarian conference on May 5 and 6, 1891, in Portsmouth, a seaport where large numbers of sailors came ashore. Gandhi and some of his fellow vegetarians including Mazmudar, with whom he came to London in 1888 on the *Clyde*, were assigned to a lodging which was a barely-disguised house of ill-fame. After the afternoon meeting of the vegetarians, Gandhi and his compatriots returned to their lodging house for dinner. Afterwards, they sat down with the hostess for a rubber of bridge. At first, the players told jokes, but then Mazmudar and the hostess began to tell indecent jokes. Gandhi joined in, but he does not explain where he learned ribald language and crude jokes. He was ready to visit one of the resident ladies when Mazmudar called out, "Whence this devil in you, my boy? Be off, quick!" Gandhi confessed that the incident in the bawdy house was the first occasion on which "a woman, other than my wife, moved me to lust."[35]

In a chapter called "The Canker of Untruth" in his *Autobiography*, Gandhi recorded a semi-sexual adventure. In his early days in England, he met in Brighton an elderly widow who took an interest in him and began to invite him to her London house each Sunday, where he was introduced to young women. Gandhi did not tell the widow that he was married with a son. Indian students in London, Gandhi wrote, were often married but hid that fact in order to "flirt with the young girls of the family in which they lived." He went on to report that the flirting was "more or less innocent."

Gandhi had become active sexually just before he was thirteen, and in England he was forced, by an oath to his mother, to be chaste for three years. He was tempted because the widow marked out for his attention a young lady who lived with her. Often Gandhi and the young woman were left alone. The widow, Gandhi speculated, had her own plans—an engagement of the two young people.

Gandhi decided to tell the widow the truth. He wrote her a letter indicating that he was sorry that he had not divulged that he was married and had a son. He assured her that he had "taken no improper liberties with the young lady."[36] This was probably true, but what sexual fantasies did he have about the young woman?

The widow responded to his frank letter, thanking him for the information about his marital state and saying that she and the young woman "had a hearty laugh over it." The Sunday meetings continued. Gandhi does not seem to have realized that the widow and the young woman may have laughed bitterly about Gandhi's confession. These women were not racists; they believed Gandhi was wealthy and a prospect for marriage.

Gandhi left London for India on June 12, 1891. At Tilbury Docks he boarded the Oceana. In three years he had fulfilled many of his objectives. He had studied for his examinations, had passed, and was now a barrister. He had perfected his spoken English and could write clearly and effectively. He had learned about English ways and current affairs from his daily reading of newspapers. He had begun to study world religions. He did not suffer discrimination because he was a man of color. He was, though, still shy in social settings and found public speaking difficult. He could now look forward to a distinguished career.

Notes

1. Gandhi, *Autobiography*, pp. 59–60; Rajmohan Gandhi, *Mohandas*, p 25.
2. Gandhi, *Autobiography*, pp. 60–61.
3. Rajmohan Gandhi, *Mohandas*, p. 28.
4. Ibid., p. 28; Gandhi, *Autobiography*, p. 61.
5. Gandhi, *Autobiography*, p. 62.
6. Ibid., p. 66. Rajmohan Gandhi, *Mohandas*, pp. 29–33; Warren S. Smith, *The London Heretics*, pp. 259–60.
7. Gandhi, *Autobiography*, p. 66.
8. Ibid., pp. 66–67; Rajmohan Gandhi, *Mohandas*, p. 32.
9. For biographical information about Henry Salt, see Stephen Winsten, *Salt and His Circle* and George Hendrick, *Henry Salt*. The quotation about the aims of the Humanitarian League is from Hendrick, *Henry Salt*, pp. 56–57.
10. Winsten and Hendrick discuss Salt's circle, which included Edward Carpenter, George Bernard Shaw, and the Webbs. In his Thoreau studies, Salt was in contact with Dr. S.A. Jones and A. W. Hosmer; see Fritz Oehlschlaeger and George Hendrick, eds., *Toward the Making of Thoreau's Modern Reputation*.
11. James D. Hunt, *Gandhi in London*, p. 15.
12. Ibid., p. 16.
13. Ibid., pp. 17–19.
14. Ibid., p. 18.
15. Ibid., pp. 18–20.
16. Ibid., pp.25–26.
17. Ibid., p. 21.
18. Payne, *Gandhi*, p. 69; Rajmohan Gandhi, *Mohandas*, pp. 33–34.
19. Gandhi, *Autobiography*. pp. 68–71.
20. Hunt, *Gandhi in London*, p. 31.
21. Ibid., pp. 31–36.
22. Gandhi, *Autobiography*, pp. 90–91; Gandhi, *The Gita According to Gandhi*, p. 126.
23. The Gandhi translation is in *The Gita According to Gandhi*, pp. 125–381. The first English translation was *The Bhagvat–Geeta*, translated by Charles Wilkins, London: C. Nourse, 1785; this was the edition used by

Emerson and Thoreau. See Arthur C. Christy, *The Orient in American Transcendentalism*, pp. 23–29 for a discussion of the *Gita*.
24. Gandhi, *The Gita According to Gandhi*, p. 127.
25. Gandhi, *Autobiography*, pp. 90–91.
26. Ibid., p. 91.
27. Hunt, *Gandhi in London*, pp. 32–33.
28. Gandhi, *Autobiography*, p. 91.
29. Ibid., p. 92.
30. Rajmohan Gandhi, *Mohandas*, p. 35; Pyarelal, *The Early Phase*, p. 211.
31. Warren S. Smith, *The London Heretics*, p. 58.
32. Gandhi, *Autobiography*. p. 50.
33. Rajmohan Gandhi, *Mohandas*, p. 45. The vegetarian articles are reprinted in the Collected Works of Mahatma Gandhi,I.
34. Gandhi, *Autobiography*, pp. 81–82; Hunt, *Gandhi in London*, pp. 22–23; 28–29.
35. Rajmohan Gandhi, *Mohandas*, p. 48
36. Gandhi, *Autobiography*, pp. 85–89.

CHAPTER III

GANDHI FACES RACISM IN SOUTH AFRICA

Gandhi, free from his law studies, spent pleasant days on the *Oceana*. At Aden, passengers for Bombay were transferred to the *Assam*. During the trip home Gandhi was concerned about three things: his troubles with his caste that had excommunicated him, his prospects in the legal profession, and his desire to be a reformer and introduce English ways into the Rajkot household. His voyage was uneventful except for rough seas after the *Assam* left Aden, and he arrived safely in Bombay in the summer of 1891.[1]

Gandhi was met by his brother Laxmidas, who told him that their mother had died not long after she had been told that he had passed his law examinations. Laxmidas had not informed him of her death, wanting to spare him "the blow in a foreign land." Gandhi's grief was greater than he had experienced after the death of his father, but he controlled his emotions: "I did not give myself up to any wild expression of grief. I could even check the tears but took to life just as though nothing had happened."[2]

Gandhi did not rush from Bombay to Rajkot to see his wife and three year old son. The reasons are not clear. In his *Autobiography*, Gandhi without explanation wrote Mehtab out of his life for the next few years, only to reintroduce him (again without giving his name) in South Africa. Since Mehtab did have contact by mail with Gandhi in London, it is possible that he was still spreading rumors about Kasturba, and Gandhi may not have wanted to see her. Dr. Mehta had already returned from London, and the Gandhi brothers stayed with him in Bombay. There Gandhi met Rajchandra, who was married to the daughter of Dr. Mehta's older brother. Rajchandra was a poet, scholar, and wealthy jeweler. His main objective in life, Gandhi wrote, "was the passion to see God face to face."[3] The two young men had serious religious conversations and became personal and spiritual friends.

Gandhi's problems with his caste still lingered. One camp in the caste wanted to readmit him and another wanted the excommunication to remain in force. Laxmidas tried to find a solution and resolve the matter. First, he took his younger brother for purification in the sacred river Godivari. Then, once the two Gandhis reached Rajkot, Laxmidas gave a caste dinner. The problem of Gandhi's exclusion was resolved except for a minority group including Kasturba's parents and Gandhi's sister Raliat and her husband. The holdouts could not entertain Gandhi, could not even give him a glass of water in their homes. Gandhi's in-laws and his sister and brother-in-law may well have looked with disfavor on him because of the shabby way he had treated Kasturba.

Gandhi deliberately did not engage in attacks on those who excommunicated him. He believed that had he provoked them, they would have retaliated. He was already trying to live amiably with those who opposed him,[4] a skill he perfected over the years.

Once he returned to Rajkot, Gandhi's relations with his wife continued to be difficult. He was still jealous, most likely because of stories Mehtab was spreading. The exact reasons for the jealousy are speculative since Gandhi chose not to disclose the specific details.

Gandhi wanted Kasturba to be able to read and write and thus be a more appropriate wife for an English-educated gentleman. Gandhi as moralist and puritan took the blame for her lack of progress: his lust got in the way. In his *Autobiography*, Gandhi seldom spoke of love or affection for his wife. For him, sexual desire was considered excessive and based on unrestrained gratification. At one time after his return from London, he sent her home to her parents, allowing her return only after he had made her miserable. Gandhi provides no details about this incident. He concluded later that this jealousy was "pure folly" on his part.[5] He seems to have learned nothing from the Mehtab-inspired jealousy of Kasturba before he left for study abroad. Mehtab may well have engineered the marital disturbance.

In the household, which included many members of the extended family, Gandhi was aided by Laxmidas in introducing European ways. Tea, coffee, cocoa, and porridge were added to the diet. Laxmidas had purchased chairs, tables, and china. European dress was being introduced. In the early days of Gandhi's return, it was believed that a European-trained barrister would gain a place in the affairs of a princely state or in the legal community. It was hoped that the finances of the large Gandhi family, depleted by Mohandas's years in England, would soon be replenished.[6]

Instead, Gandhi appeared to be a white elephant. He did not know Indian law, meaning he could hardly build a practice in Rajkot. He had no friends in high places to help him gain a state appointment. He decided to go to Bombay to gain experience in the High Court and to study Indian law. He could then begin to get briefs.

In November of 1891, Gandhi moved to Bombay. He had returned to India only a few months earlier. He did not take his wife and son with him. He set up housekeeping with a Brahman cook who could not cook and could not keep himself or the food clean. Gandhi was observing in the courts and reading Indian law but was receiving no briefs. He had a great deal of spare time and tried to teach the servant to cook and to clean, but failed. He then took on some of those duties himself, and the two men went on merrily together, inter-dining (Gandhi was of a lower caste) and running up expenses.[7] Gandhi's description of this interlude seems to indicate that he preferred this bachelor life to marriage. There was no jealousy, no sex. This brief idyll lasted only a few months.

Gandhi was learning that it would be years before he could support himself. He was apprehensive about appearing in court, but he was given a fee of 30 rupees to represent a defendant in Small Causes Court. When he arose to examine the witnesses for the plaintiff, he was struck dumb. His head was reeling, and he thought the courtroom was doing likewise. He could think of no questions to ask. In disgrace, he left the court after telling the agent that the fee was to be returned, and another pleader was brought in.[8]

Though he seemed to have no future in the courtroom, he did draft a memorial for a poor man in Porbandar whose land had been confiscated. He was not charging for his work. Gandhi found he possessed one skill: he wrote with precision and produced an excellent memorial. With a sense of humor, Gandhi remarked: "My business would flourish if I drafted memorials without any fees."[9]

Gandhi heard of a job teaching English but was rejected because he was not a B.A. graduate. After six months he closed up his accommodations in Bombay and returned to Rajkot. He then had some minor financial success drafting applications and memorials, assignments sent to him by Laxmidas, a pleader, and his brother's partner. He does not mention his reunion with his wife and son.

Against his will, Gandhi was caught up in the affairs of the princely state of Porbandar. Laxmidas had been secretary and advisor to the young heir to the throne, and it was alleged that Laxmidas had known about the young man's theft of state jewels but had taken no action. The British Agent E. C. K. Ollivant was investigating the charge which had placed Laxmidas under a cloud of suspicion. Mohandas had met Ollivant in England and had found him pleasant. Laxmidas urged his younger brother to go to Olli-

Gandhi Faces Racism in South Africa

vant and plead Laxmidas's case. Laxmidas would not listen to his brother's objections, and Mohandas reluctantly made an appointment to see Ollivant.

Gandhi reminded the British Agent of their acquaintance in England. The reminder seemed to stiffen the Britisher, and Gandhi read his reaction to mean, "Surely you have not come here to abuse that acquaintance, have you?" Gandhi began to talk about Laxmidas's problem, and the Agent was impatient: "Your brother is an intriguer. I want to hear nothing more from you, I have no time. If your brother has anything to say, let him apply through the proper channel."

Gandhi did not desist. He went on with his defense of Laxmidas.

"You must go now."

"But please hear me out," which made Ollivant even more angry. He called his peon (attendant) to take Gandhi out.

The peon put his hands on Gandhi's shoulders and escorted him out of the room.[10]

Both Ollivant and Gandhi were wrong. Gandhi knew that he should not have been arguing his brother's case. Ollivant was arrogant, as the Agents with their strong racist views, tended to be when dealing with Indians.

Gandhi immediately wrote Ollivant: "You have insulted me. You have assaulted me through your peon. If you make no amends, I shall have to proceed against you."[11] Gandhi mistakenly believed that he and Ollivant had equal rights in the Empire. Ollivant knew better; Indians were at best second class citizens ruled by the British Raj. Gandhi was a long time learning that truth.

Ollivant responded that Gandhi was rude to him and would not leave; therefore, he asked his peon to remove him. "You are at liberty," Ollivant wrote, "to proceed as you wish." Gandhi did not know what to do, but Sir Pherozeshah Mehta, upon reviewing the documents, advised through an intermediary that "such things are the common experience of many *vakils* (pleaders) and barristers. He (Gandhi) is still fresh from England and hot-blooded. He does not know British officers. If he would earn something and have an easy time here, let him tear up the note and pocket the insult." He concluded: "Tell him he has yet to know life."[12]

The advice to go along to get along was as bitter as wormwood to Gandhi. He did not proceed against Ollivant, but he was determined never again to try to exploit friendship. He was not willing to give in meekly and curry favor with Ollivant, who had great power in the judicial and political systems. His legal practice was in danger if he were out of favor with the Agent, and his prospects of a Prime Ministership seemed destroyed. Gandhi was beginning to understand the corrupt Raj system, but he was reluctant to acknowledge what he knew.

The atmosphere in Rajkot was poisonous, but suddenly Gandhi was offered a way out. Laxmidas helped him obtain a position with the Muslim merchant firm Dada Abdulla & Company in South Africa. That successful firm had many financial interests and was highly profitable.[13]

This one-year appointment in South Africa was to be a lucrative one; all Gandhi's expenses were to be paid, and his salary was £105. Sheth Abdul Karim Jhaveri, partner in the firm, was in Porbandar and told Gandhi: "It won't be a difficult job. We have big Europeans as our friends, whose acquaintance you will make. You can be useful to us in our shop. Much of our correspondence is in English and you can help us with that too."[14] The firm already had European barristers, and Gandhi would be a glorified clerk.

Gandhi should have been told about the racism in the four colonies which were eventually united in 1910 as the Union of South Africa. Beginning in 1860, indentured Indian laborers came to Natal to work in the cane fields, and over the years more Indians came to South African colonies. In the two British-dominated colonies, Natal and the Cape; and the two Dutch (Boer) ones, the Orange Free State and the Transvaal. Indians were discriminated against on trains and stage-coaches, in schools, hotels and restaurants, and in some cases they were forced off sidewalks. They faced harsh taxes, and there were efforts to deport to India indentured workers who had completed their terms or service.[15] Gandhi defended Sheth Abdul Karim Jhaveri, saying he "was a frank, simple man, ignorant of the real state of affairs. He had no idea of the hardships to which Indians were subjected in Natal."[16] Gandhi liked to think the best of people, but it seems unlikely that a partner in a firm with large-scale business in South Africa would not know about racism in Natal and the other colonies.

Gandhi wrote in his *Autobiography* that he had some distress in parting from his wife. A second son had been born since his return from London. "Our love," he wrote, "could not yet be called free from lust, but it was getting gradually purer."[17] Gandhi continued to believe that sexual activity was lustful and evil.

As part of his role as Anglo-Indian gentleman, Gandhi travelled first class, but the *Safari* he was to sail on had already assigned all its first-class berths. Gandhi went to the chief officer, asking to be squeezed in. There was an extra berth in the chief officer's cabin, and Gandhi agreed to take it. The *Safari* departed Bombay on April 19, 1893.

Gandhi was developing an outgoing personality, and he soon became friends with the captain, who taught him to play chess. The captain was a novice player and Gandhi, a beginner, was a desirable opponent.[18]

At Zanzibar, the captain invited Gandhi and an Englishman to go with him on an outing. Gandhi was naive and did not know the three were going to the "Negro women's quarters." Each man was shown into a room, and Gandhi was "dumb with shame." He still kept the vow he had made his mother, but he pitied himself "for not having the courage to refuse to go into the room."[19]

At Zanzibar, Gandhi changed to the *Admiral* for the last leg of the trip to Durban, where he debarked on May 23, 1893. As he left the ship, Gandhi was wearing a frock coat, striped trousers, and watch and chain, and a black turban.[20] His appearance was completely different from the Muslim merchants who chose loose fitting white garments and wore heavy beards Gandhi immediately realized that he was a figure of curiosity, and that Abdulla Sheth, partner in the firm, who met him, was treated snobbishly by Europeans. Abdulla Sheth was a wealthy businessman, but he was a man of color.[21]

Abdulla Sheth was at first distressed by Gandhi, whose style of dress and European ways he felt would be expensive for the firm to support. And could this man be trusted? Abdulla Sheth was by nature suspicious, and Gandhi does not indicate how he overcame Abdulla Sheth's doubts. In his *Autobiography*, Gandhi is silent about his first two or three days in Durban. Then Abdulla Sheth took Gandhi to observe a court session. He introduced Gandhi to several people and had him sit next to one of the company's attorneys. The magistrate kept looking at Gandhi and finally asked him to remove his turban. Gandhi refused and left the courtroom.[22] Gandhi would not pocket the insult.

Abdulla Sheth's explanation of why some from India were asked to remove their turbans introduced Gandhi to many customs of the country. Those wearing Muslim dress were allowed to keep their turbans on; they called themselves "Arabs" and had paid their own way to Natal. Most Indians came as indentured laborers and were forced to remove their head coverings. Gandhi realized the request to remove his turban was an insult, and he thought he might, instead, wear a hat. Abdulla Sheth explained that many of the Indians who wore hats were children of indentured laborers who had remained in Natal at the end of their indenture. Many of these Indians were converts to Christianity and served as waiters. Abdulla Sheth argued that Gandhi did not want to be mistaken for a waiter, and that he should not wear a hat because it would "compromise those insisting on wearing Indian turbans."[23] Gandhi also learned that the Parsis in Natal called themselves Persians in order to obtain better treatment from Europeans.

Gandhi Faces Racism in South Africa

Indians were routinely called "coolies," (that is, porters), a derogatory term used throughout the four colonies in South Africa. Gandhi was a "coolie barrister." Many of the Indians who had come as indentured laborers were Tamil, and "sami" was a suffix on many of their names. The word "sami" is a form of "Swami," meaning a master. Europeans used "sami" as a derogatory term, not recognizing that they were in fact using a term of praise for the Indian called that term.[24] At this same time in the South, black people were routinely called "nigger."

Gandhi's South African education was only beginning. He wrote a local newspaper about his experiences in court and defended his wearing a turban. His letter created some heated discussions, and Gandhi was called an "unwelcome visitor."[25] For the next two decades, most Europeans in the colonies considered him "unwelcome."

In the days after the turban episode, Gandhi was engaged in extensive study. He learned that the lawsuit that brought him to Durban had to do largely with accounting practices. Gandhi knew nothing about that subject, but he acquired a basic text on bookkeeping and quickly mastered it.[26] Throughout the next decades, he was able to concentrate on a subject and learn all the relevant facts.

On the seventh or eighth day Gandhi was in Natal, he left for Pretoria to assist in the lawsuit between Abdulla Sheth and his relative Tyeb Sheth. Pretoria was in the Transvaal, and the racial situation there was even more dire for Indians than it was in Natal. Gandhi at the time of his departure was still innocent about the extent of racism in the four colonies.

The company arranged for Gandhi to have a first class ticket. Usually first class passengers paid an extra five shillings for bedding. Gandhi out of "obstinacy and pride" decided against bedding—he had some with him. Abdulla Sheth knew the dangers of calling attention to oneself in these racist colonies. He said to Gandhi: "Look, now, this is a different country from India. Thank God, we have enough and to spare. Please do not stint yourself in anything that you may need."[27] Gandhi thanked him, and in his ignorance told him not to be anxious.

At first, Gandhi faced no problems on the train. About 9 p. m., though, the train arrived in Maritzburg, and an employee of the railway company came in to ask if Gandhi wished to be supplied with bedding. Gandhi declined. Then a passenger came in, looked at the Indian in a first class compartment, and saw that he was "colored." The passenger went out, only to return with officials, one of whom said, "Come along, you must go to the van compartment."

Gandhi responded: "But I have a first class ticket."

Another official said: "That doesn't matter. I tell you, you must go to the van compartment."

"I tell you, I was permitted to travel in this compartment at Durban, and I insist on going on in it."

"No you won't. You must leave this compartment, or else I shall have to call a police constable to push you out."

"Yes, you may. I refuse to get out voluntarily." The constable came, took Gandhi's hand, and pushed him out, along with his baggage.[28]

****

African Americans faced similar situations in the nineteenth and well into the twentieth century. Frederick Douglass, an escaped slave living in Massachusetts, was ordered into a "Jim Crow" car on the railroad on September 8, 1841. Douglass was seated with his friend John A. Collins, a white man, who remonstrated against the segregation policy of the company. Douglass and Collins refused to move. The conductor left the car but returned with "four or five of the Company's minions," ready to take action. The company workers "like so many hyenas," snaked Douglass out of his seat and thrust him into the "negro car," with a "Go there, that's good enough for you, d--n you."

Gandhi Faces Racism in South Africa 41

On December 1, 1955, Rosa Parks in Montgomery, Alabama, was on her way home from work as a seamstress in a department store.

Riding a bus in the former Confederate states was difficult for blacks. The drivers of city buses had people of color enter the front door, pay the fee, depart and then enter the rear door. Often the bus pulled away before the patron could reach the back entrance. Rosa Parks entered the bus and sat down in a colored section. To her dismay, she saw the driver was James F. Blake, who had put her off a bus many years previously. The white section filled, and Blake called for blacks to stand up to give a seat to a white man. At first, nobody moved. Blake called out, "Y'll better make it light on yourselves and let me have those seats." Other blacks moved; Rosa Parks did not; she later explained: "I had no idea that history was being made. I was just tired of giving in. Somehow, I felt that what I did was right by standing up to that bus driver....I knew that I could have been lynched, manhandled, or beaten when the police came. I chose not to move. When I made that decision, I knew that I had the strength of my ancestors with me."

Mrs. Parks was arrested. Out of the black protest movement that followed, the Rev. Dr. Martin Luther King, Jr. came to prominence.[29]

****

It was a bitterly cold night. Gandhi was left sitting in an unheated waiting room. His overcoat was in his luggage, sequestered by the local railway authorities, and he was afraid to ask for his overcoat. Now he knew he had been insulted. He sat shivering in the dark room. A passenger came in at midnight, but Gandhi was in no mood to talk. Gandhi considered himself a gentleman, an educated man, a devoted supporter of Victoria, Empress of India. How should such a man react to discrimination? Gandhi in his *Autobiography* reconstructed his thoughts that cold night in Maritzburg:

Should I fight for my rights or go back to India, or should I go on to Pretoria without minding the insults, and return to India after finishing the case? It would be cowardice to run back to India without fulfilling my obligation. The hardship to which I was subjected was superficial—only a symptom of the deep disease of colour prejudice. I should try, if possible, to root out the disease and suffer hardships in the process. Redress for wrongs I should seek only to the extent that would be necessary for the removal of the colour prejudice.[30] Gandhi decided he must go on to Pretoria, but he still had not fully realized how ingrained color prejudice was in South Africa.

Erik H. Erikson in his provocative *Gandhi's Truth* wrote about the Maritzburg episode: "There is every reason to believe that the central identity which here found its historical time and place was the conviction [of Gandhi] that among Indians in South Africa he was the only person equipped by fate to reform a situation which under no condition could be tolerated."[31]

Based on incomplete knowledge of the color bar in South Africa, Gandhi was thinking of the first steps which would eventually lead to large-scale nonviolent civil disobedience. He may or may not have thought of himself in the terms used by Erikson, but he did see himself as working with the legal system to bring about changes in discriminatory laws.

The next morning Gandhi sent a long telegram to the General Manager of the railway company about his treatment the night before, and he also informed Abdulla Sheth about those events. Abdulla Sheth then met with the General Manager, who defended the actions of railway authorities, but the General Manager also instructed the Station Master in Maritzburg to make certain that the passenger reached his destination safely.

Abdulla Sheth sent telegrams to Indian merchants in Maritzburg and surrounding towns asking them to see Gandhi at the station, where he was waiting for the night train. The merchants arrived and told Gandhi their hardships and "tales of woe," which gave Gandhi new information about segregation but was hardly comforting. Going into the second week in Natal, Gandhi had not yet met indentured laborers, with their own, more severe, tales of hardship and mistreatment.

Gandhi Faces Racism in South Africa

When the night train arrived, Gandhi was shown to his reserved berth. He had learned not to call special attention to himself and bought the five shilling bedding ticket. The actions of the General Manager resulted in this part of Gandhi's trip proceeding without incident, but Gandhi was not so fortunate at the next stop.[32]

The train reached Charlestown, but there was no rail line yet to Johannesburg. Gandhi needed to take the stage-coach, which would stop at Standerton at night before continuing on. He had a ticket, but it was for the previous day. The agent declared that the ticket had been cancelled. Without a valid ticket, "coolie" Gandhi was not to be seated with the European passengers inside. Once again, Gandhi was ordered to suffer an injustice. He knew that if he stayed behind, wired the General Manager of the stage-coach company and waited for a response, he might be delayed several days. He decided to pocket the insult.

Gandhi was seated outside on the coachbox. The leader (conductor) generally sat there with the driver, but he decided to sit inside the coach. When the coach reached Pardekoph in the Transvaal at about 3 o'clock that afternoon, the leader wanted to smoke and decided to reclaim his seat on the coachbox. He took a piece of dirty sacking, spread it on the footboard, and addressed Gandhi: "Sami, you sit on this. I want to sit near the driver."

Gandhi replied in fear and trembling: "It was you who seated me here, though I should have been accommodated inside. I put up with the insult. Now that you want to sit outside and smoke, you would have me sit at your feet. I will not do so, but I am prepared to sit inside."

During Gandhi's protest, the leader began to box the "coolie's" ears. He then seized Gandhi's arm and tried to drag him down. Gandhi held tight to the brass rails of the coachbox. Gandhi was determined to keep his place even if his wrist bones were broken.

The passengers were watching the strong leader belabor, with curses, the well-dressed small brown man who was asserting his rights. Some of the passengers called out, "Man, leave him alone. Don't beat him. He is not to blame. He is right. If he can't stay there, let him come and sit with us."[33] Gandhi was learning that some Europeans were sympathetic.

"No fear," the leader called out, but he was crestfallen that the passengers did not approve his actions, and he stopped beating Gandhi. He continued to swear at the coolie, and then pointed to a Khoikhoi (Hottentot) who had also been sitting in the coachbox with Gandhi and the driver, told him to sit on the sack, took the now vacant seat, and sent Gandhi inside the coach. Gandhi was not certain he would reach his destination alive. The leader cast angry looks at him and said, "Take care, let me once get to Standerton and I shall show you what I do." Gandhi knew there would be ample time for reprisals during the overnight stop.

The stage coach did not reach Standerton until dark. Dada Abdulla had sent a telegram alerting Indians to Gandhi's arrival, and the mistreated passenger was met and taken to the shop of Sheth Isa Haji Sumer. Gandhi told his host and his clerks about the difficulties he had experienced the past days, and they told Gandhi about their own "bitter experiences."[34]

****

Frederick Douglass on September 28, 1841, once again boarded a car on the Eastern Railroad. The same conductor who had previously sent him to a Jim Crow car once again ordered Douglass to leave the coach and ride in a Jim Crow car. Douglass refused. A friend of Douglass then said: "Can't I ride with him, if he goes into the forward car?"

Conductor: "No. I'd as soon haul you out of his car as I'd haul him from this."

Douglass: "There are but very few in this car, and why, since no objection has been made, do you order me out?"

Passenger: "I've no objection to ride with him—let's take a vote on the question."

Gandhi Faces Racism in South Africa 45

The conductor refused to take a vote, and when asked his reasons for sending Douglass to the Jim Crow car, "finally made up his mind to say, in a half-suppressed, half-audible voice, 'Because you are black.'"

Railway employees were called to remove Douglass, and five or six of them laid hands on him, but he was firmly attached to the seat. The seat gave way, and Douglass and a companion seated with him were deposited on the ground.[35]

****

Gandhi wrote a letter to the agent of the stage-coach company about the threat made by the leader. The agent responded that the coach to be used the next day was larger, that Gandhi had a seat inside, and that the leader who threatened Gandhi would not be on duty. The stage-coach left the next morning, and Gandhi reached Johannesburg without incident.

The Indian who was to meet Gandhi at the Johannesburg station apparently did not recognize the barrister, and Gandhi took a cab to the Grand National Hotel, where he asked the Manager for a room. The Manager was polite but firm: "I am very sorry, we are full up." Then Gandhi took a cab to an Indian's shop, where he was greeted by Sheth Abdul Gani, who laughed when told about the incident at the hotel:

"How ever did you expect to be admitted to a hotel?"

"Why not?" Gandhi responded, still not comprehending the pervasive racism in the four colonies.

Sheth Adbul Gani spoke with fervor: "You will come to know after you have stayed here a few days. Only we can live in a land like this, because, for making money, we do not mind pocketing insults, and here we are. This country is not for men like you. Look now, you have to go to Pretoria tomorrow. You will have to travel third class. Conditions in the Transvaal are worse than in Natal. First and second class tickets are never issued to Indians."

Gandhi asked if efforts had been made to end this discrimination on trains and stage-coaches. Sheth Abdul Gani responded: "We have sent representations, but I confess our own men do not want as a rule to travel first or second."

Gandhi refused to accept segregated travel. He wrote the Station Master that he was a barrister and always travelled first class. He needed to reach Pretoria quickly, and since there was not time enough for him to receive a reply he would go directly to the station to purchase his ticket. Gandhi hoped that his being dressed as an Anglo-Indian gentleman—he wore a frock coat and a necktie—would help convince the agent to provide him with a first class ticket.

Gandhi had found support from European passengers on the stage-coach when he was being assaulted by the leader. He found another sympathizer in the Station Master, who said, "I am not a Transvaaler. I am a Hollander. I appreciate your feelings, and you have my sympathy. I do want to give you a ticket—on one condition, however, that, if the guard should ask you to shift to the third class, you will not involve me in the affair, by which I mean that you should not proceed against the Railway Company. I wish you a safe journey. I can see you are a gentleman."

The first class ticket was issued.[36]

Sheth Abdul Gani had accompanied Gandhi to the station. He was surprised that Gandhi was issued a first class ticket, but he warned, "I shall be thankful if you reach Pretoria all right. I am afraid the guard will not leave you in peace in the first class and even if he does, the passengers will not."

After the train left the station, the guard came to examine tickets. He was angry to see a man of color in first class and motioned for Gandhi to go to the third class car. Gandhi produced his ticket, but the guard was adamant, "That doesn't matter; remove to the third class."

Gandhi Faces Racism in South Africa

The only other person in the compartment was an Englishman, who addressed the guard, "What do you mean by troubling the gentleman? Don't you see he has a first class ticket? I do not mind in the least his travelling with me." The Englishman addressed Gandhi, "You should make yourself comfortable where you are."

The guard responded, "If you want to travel with a coolie, what do I care?"[37]

Gandhi encountered no more problems during the thirty-seven mile train trip to Pretoria, but his travel difficulties were not over. He was not met at the station and was reluctant to ask directions to a small hotel, for he feared being insulted. He did speak to the ticket collector who was courteous but not really of help. An African American, probably a tout, spoke up: "I see that you are an utter stranger here, without any friends. If you will come with me, I will take you to a small hotel, of which the proprietor is an American who is very well known to me. I think he will accept you."

Gandhi had doubts about the offer, for he was learning that the color bar kept him from staying in European hotels. The two men went to Johnston's Family Hotel, and after the African American conferred with the owner, Mr. Johnston agreed to accept Gandhi for the night if his guest would agree to have dinner served to him in his room. "I assure you that I have no colour prejudice. But I have only European custom, and, if I allowed you to eat in the dining room, my guests might be offended and even go away."

Gandhi agreed to the condition.

In his room, Gandhi waited for a waiter to bring his meal. Instead, Mr. Johnston appeared, saying, "I was ashamed of having asked you to have your dinner here. So I spoke to the other guests about you, and asked them if they would mind your having your dinner in the dining room. They said they had no objection, and that they did not mind your staying here as long as you liked. Please, therefore, come to the dining room, if you will, and stay here as long as you wish."[38]

After a night in the hotel, Gandhi met with Mr. A.W. Baker, one of the attorneys for Dada Abdulla Company. Baker greeted Gandhi warmly; yet there was an air of condescension—though Gandhi does not seem to have recognized it—as Baker said: "We have no work for you here as barrister, for we have engaged the best counsel." He had also not found rooms for Gandhi, since the color prejudice in the Transvaal was particularly strong, but he knew a poor woman, a baker's wife, who would take Gandhi in. There is no indication that Baker considered having Gandhi stay with him. Nor did he make inquiries about placing Gandhi in a small hotel or a well-regarded boarding house. Baker did indicate that he would ask, through Gandhi, for all the legal information he needed from the merchant firm.

Baker was a lay preacher, and he quickly turned from legal matters to questioning Gandhi about his religious views. Gandhi's response indicated he was a seeker, a Hindu who knew little about his religion or other world religions. He said he was going to make a study of Hinduism and other religions. That response was not quite accurate, for Gandhi in London had already studied the Bhagavad-Gita, Theosophy, Buddhism, and Christianity. Baker seems to have been impressed with that answer, but he was more interested in the study of Christianity. Baker then asked Gandhi to join a daily five minute prayer session, where he would meet congenial friends. Baker promised to give Gandhi religious books to read, including the Holy Bible.

Baker took Gandhi to the house of a commercial baker and introduced him to the baker's wife. Baker then spoke to her privately, and she agreed to take Gandhi as a roomer at 35 shillings a week. Gandhi returned to the hotel, moved his belongings to his new residence, and had a vegetarian lunch there. The family was working class, and Gandhi found them to be congenial. He does not indicate whether they were Europeans without color prejudice or Indians. A.W. Baker had his own prejudices in sending Gandhi to live with the family of a baker instead of taking him into his own home. Gandhi, though, adapted to this insult.

Gandhi Faces Racism in South Africa

That night Gandhi mused on his conversation with Baker about religion. What was the meaning of Baker's interest in him? How extensively should he study Christianity? Where would he find Hindu texts? He seemingly did not have with him Sir Edwin Arnold's translation of the *Gita* called *The Song Celestial* or any Hindu texts. He speculated that he could not understand Christianity without first knowing Hinduism. He seems to have understood, but was reluctant to admit, that Baker looked upon him as a prize convert.[39]

Gandhi began to attend the noon prayer meetings, and there he met several agreeable people who were not color prejudiced, including two elderly women studying Zulu in preparation for mission work in Swaziland. They invited Gandhi to Sunday afternoon tea, where he met Michael Coates, a Quaker who loaned Christian books to Gandhi and who read Gandhi's religious diary. Although Coates was un-Quaker like in his low regard for Hinduism, he and Gandhi became friends. It is obvious, though, that Gandhi's new acquaintances were all working toward making a high-profile convert.

Coates introduced Gandhi to other Christians, including a family of Plymouth Brethren, one of whom argued to Gandhi that all people were sinful, but Jesus had atoned for the sins of all mankind. Mankind, therefore, should give up brooding about sin, accept Jesus, and in this new state of salvation go on with life without anguish. Gandhi responded that he could not accept that version of Christianity: "I do not seek redemption from the consequences of my sin. I seek to be redeemed from sin itself, or rather from the very thought of sin."[40]

During his first year in South Africa Gandhi attended the Wellington Convention, an interdenominational evangelical meeting in Cape Town. There was pressure to convert, but he resisted. He did not believe that "Jesus was the only incarnate son of God and that only he who believed in him would have everlasting life." He also did not believe Hinduism was a perfect religion. He realized that sects, castes, and untouchability were clearly defects in that religion. He did read Hindu texts, including

Panchikaran, Maniratnamala, and others. The book that impressed him most during this period of study of world religions was Tolstoy's *The Kingdom of God Is Within You,* which overwhelmed him. He praised "the independent thinking, profound morality, and the truthfulness" of the work.[41]

While living in Pretoria, Gandhi set out to meet every Indian in the city and learn their experiences. Most of the Indians in the Transvaal were Muslim merchants, though there were a few Hindus in residence. He called a meeting of Indians, and for the first time was not shy or hesitant when he spoke. He urged the merchants who were often regarded as untrustworthy by Europeans to be truthful in their business dealings. The merchants argued that "pure truth was out of the question in business." Gandhi wanted the merchants to realize that if they were regarded as duplicitous, their conduct would color the European perception of all Indians. In the discussions that followed, he urged Indians to learn English, and he began to tutor three men—a barber, a clerk, and a shopkeeper.[42] He was now meeting working people in addition to merchants, but he still had not talked to indentured laborers, who were being held in semi-slavery and kept away from anyone who might be a rabble-rouser.

Gandhi was learning the problems of small business owners, clerks, and workers such as barbers, and their difficulties were often greater than those faced by wealthy merchants. Gandhi did address several aspects of discrimination. He protested the treatment of Indians on railroads and was told that first and second class tickets were available to Indians properly dressed.[43] While this was seemingly a concession, the Station Master was to make the decision on proper dress. Gandhi in his European-style garb would likely pass, but a Muslim merchant in loose-fitting white garments might not.

By the end of his first year in Pretoria, Gandhi knew the Indians there, and they knew him. He was, in his own way, studying the social, economic, and political conditions in that part of South Africa. He was the most highly educated Indian in Pretoria, and he felt confident as he met and talked with his fellow Indians who had little formal training.

The law case itself was complicated, and Gandhi's study of bookkeeping allowed him to understand its intricacies. He decided that his employer was likely to prevail, but only after protracted litigation. It was to the advantage of barristers on both sides of the case to have the litigation go on and on. From his first days in South Africa, Gandhi had suggested settling the case out of court.[44] He approached Tyeb, suggesting arbitration. Largely because of rising legal expenses, both sides finally agreed to this approach. In the arbitration, Dada Abdulla and Company was awarded £37,000 and costs. It was not possible for Tyeb to pay that large sum all at once, and he would have been forced into bankruptcy. Gandhi proposed a solution: Tyeb would be allowed to make payments over a number of years. Barrister Gandhi had been brought to South Africa as an English-speaking clerk to help the European barristers employed by Dada Abdulla and Company, but he was the one instrumental in settling the lawsuit. Characteristically, he did not brag about his lawyerly skills.

Gandhi in his *Autobiography* made specific comments about what he had learned in the settlement of this difficult dispute: "I had learnt the true practice of law. I had learnt to find out the better side of human nature and to enter men's hearts. I realized that the true function of a lawyer was to unite parties riven asunder."[45]

During the next twenty years in South Africa, Gandhi worked to bring about compromises. His belief in uniting warring parties was a part of the method of nonviolent disobedience to unjust laws he was to develop in the coming years. He appealed to the better natures of his adversaries.

With the Dada Abdulla-Tyeb lawsuit concluded, Gandhi must leave South Africa. He had suffered indignities because of color prejudice, and he had learned about many of the problems his fellow Indians faced in the four colonies. Indian merchants lauded his abilities as a lawyer but made no efforts to keep him from returning to India. At the end of May,

1894, Gandhi was in Durban getting ready to leave for Bombay. Abdulla Sheth gave him a farewell party. During the day-long festivities Gandhi came across a newspaper article under the caption "Indian Franchise" concerning a bill before the legislature that would deprive Indians of their right to vote to elect members of the Natal legislature. Gandhi, having been residing in Pretoria, knew nothing of the bill, and the guests at his farewell party were also unaware of it.

Gandhi asked Abdulla Sheth about the bill. Abdulla Sheth responded: "What can we understand of these matters? We can only understand things that affect our trade. As you know all our trade in the Orange Free State has been swept away. We agitated about it, but in vain. We are after all lame men, being unlettered. We generally take in newspapers simply to ascertain the daily market rates, etc. What can we know of legislation? Our eyes and ears are the European attorneys here."

Gandhi answered: "But there are so many young Indians born and educated here. Do they not help you?" (Gandhi was apparently thinking of Indians educated in mission schools.) Abdulla Sheth (in despair) responded: "They! They never care to come to us, and to tell you the truth, we care less to recognize them. Being Christians, they are under the thumb of the white clergymen, who in their turn are subject to the Government."

Gandhi had his own questions about Indians and Christianity, but he was leaving for India and did not want to discuss that matter with Abdulla Sheth. Instead, he said, "This Bill, if it passes into law, will make our lot extremely difficult. It is the first nail into our coffin. It strikes at the root of our self-respect."

Abdulla Sheth replied: "It may." He then explained the genesis of the problem: Harry Escombe, a European attorney for the firm, had been in an election against a wharf engineer. Escombe had advised Indians to register, and they voted for him, causing European resentment against Indians. Abdulla Sheth continued, "Well, then, what is your advice?"

Some of the guests were listening to the conversation, and one had a specific suggestion: "You cancel your passage by this boat, stay here a month longer, and we will fight as you direct us."

Another guest chimed in with, "Abdulla Sheth, you must detain" the barrister.

Abdulla Sheth then proposed: "I may not detain him now. Or rather, you have as much right as I to do so....Let us all persuade him to stay on. But you should remember that he is a barrister. What about his fees?"

Gandhi, embarrassed about the mention of compensation, protested: "Abdulla Sheth, fees are out of the question. There can be no fees for public work. I can stay, if at all, as a servant....I am prepared to stay a month longer. There is one thing, however. Though you need not pay me anything, work of the nature we contemplate cannot be done without some funds to start with. And it is clear that one man is not enough for this work. Many must come forward to help him."

A chorus of voices answered: "Allah is great and merciful. Money will come in. Men there are, as many as you may need. You please consent to stay and all will be well." There was a tide of optimism by those who had little knowledge of the problems they faced.[46]

Notes

1. Rajmohan Gandhi, *Mohandas*, pp. 51–53; Gandhi, *Autobiography*. p. 111.
2. Gandhi, *Autobiography*, pp. 111–12.
3. Ibid., p. 113.
4. Ibid., pp. 115–16; Rajmohan Gandhi, *Mohandas*, p. 54.
5. Gandhi, *Autobiography*, p. 116.
6. Ibid., p. 117.
7. Ibid., pp. 117–18; Rajmohan Gandhi, *Mohandas*, pp. 55.
8. Gandhi, *Autobiography*, p. 120.
9. Ibid., p. 121.
10. Ibid., pp. 124–25.
11. Ibid., p. 125.
12. Ibid., pp. 125–26.
13. Rajmohan Gandhi, *Mohandas*, p. 61; Gandhi, *Autobiography* 128–29.
14. Gandhi, *Autobiography*, p. 129.
15. Gandhi, *Satyagraha in South Africa*, pp. 38–63; *Collected Works of Mahatma Gandhi*, I:xxi–xxv.
16. Gandhi, *Satyagraha in South Africa*, p. 68.
17. Gandhi, *Autobiography*, p. 130.
18. Ibid., p. 130–31; Rajmohan Gandhi, *Mohandas*, pp. 62–63.
19. Gandhi, *Autobiography*, p. 132.
20. Rajmohan Gandhi, *Mohandas*, p. 63, Gandhi, *Satyagraha in South Africa*, p. 68.
21. Gandhi, *Autobiography*, p. 134.
22. Ibid., p. 135.
23. Ibid., p. 136–37.
24. Ibid., p. 136.
25. Ibid., p. 137
26. Ibid., pp. 138–39.
27. Ibid., p. 140.
28. Ibid., pp. 140–41.
29. The account of Douglass's troubles on a New England railroad is reproduced in Hendrick and Hendrick, *Why Not Every Man?*; see pp. 56–58. See Douglas Brinkley, *Rosa Parks*, for Mrs. Parks's arrest, her reaction is in her *Quiet Strength*, pp. 23–24.
30. Gandhi, *Autobiography*, p. 141.

31. Erik H. Erikson, *Gandhi's Truth*, p. 166.
32. Gandhi, *Autobiography*, pp. 141–42.
33. Ibid., p. 143.
34. Ibid., pp. 144–45.
35. The account of Douglass's second problem on a railroad is from Hendrick and Hendrick, *Why Not Every Man?*, pp. 58–62.
36. Gandhi, *Autobiography*, pp. 145–47.
37. Ibid., pp. 147–48.
38. Ibid., pp. 149–50.
39. Ibid., pp. 151–52.
40. Ibid., pp. 153–56.
41. Ibid., pp. 170–72; see also James D. Hunt, *Gandhi and the Nonconformists*, pp. 32–35.
42. Gandhi, *Autobiography*, pp. 157–58.
43. Ibid., pp. 157–59.
44. Ibid., pp. 139. 167.
45. Ibid., p. 168.
46. Ibid., pp. 173–75.

Chapter IV

Gandhi's Early Experiences in Natal

Gandhi immediately set to work organizing against the Natal bill to disenfranchise Indians then pending in the legislature. He quickly put together a group of Muslim merchants, Christian Indians, Hindus, and Parsis to work against the proposed legislation. In his study of world religions, Gandhi had come to find virtues in every religion, and this made it easier for him, at first, to build a coalition.

The first order of business was to send a telegram to the Speaker of the Natal Assembly asking that discussion of the bill be postponed. The Speaker agreed to a two day delay. Gandhi then oversaw the drafting of a petition to be presented to the Assembly asking that the bill not be passed. Merchants sent carriages out with helpers to gather needed signatures for the petition. With large-scale volunteer help, the petition was presented within two days. As the most knowledgeable knew, it was a foregone conclusion that the bill would pass, for the anti-Indian bias was strong in the colony. Still, the Indian community had become more unified and was ready to insist on its political rights.

In a brilliant tactical move, Gandhi then prepared a petition to send to Lord Ripon, Secretary of State for the Colonies, in London, arguing that Indians had the right to the franchise. Again, in short order, signatures were gathered—10,000 of them—and the petition was sent. Gandhi had a thousand copies printed, and these copies were distributed broadly, with special attention to newspapers and to individuals interested in Indian affairs. The *Times of India* and the *London Times* wrote favorably about the Indian cause. Gandhi had no models for political protest before him and was improvising. He clearly understood that he needed to gain support from leading newspapers. He was also showing rare skills as an administrator and in analyzing and describing the problems faced by Indians in South Africa. He was also successful in securing financial support and in finding volunteers to do the work of gathering materials and signatures, copying documents, and making mass mailings.[1]

Gandhi's efforts were partially successfully. The £25 proposed tax was eventually reduced to £3, still prohibitive for poorly-paid Indians. New Indian applicants wishing to register to vote were excluded, but those already on the voting list could continue to vote.[2]

****

After the end of Reconstruction in 1877, African Americans in the former Confederate states were subjected to a similar loss in voting rights. By the 1890s most African Americans had been struck from the voting rolls by way of poll taxes or tests on the Constitution; African Americans almost always were declared to have failed the tests. These voting restrictions continued into the 1950s.

Rosa Parks, the black heroine of the Civil Rights movement, went to work in 1941 at Maxwell Field just outside of Montgomery, Alabama, where she lived and where African Americans were kept from voting. President Franklin D. Roosevelt had forbidden racial segregation on military bases. Public transportation on base was integrated, but as soon as Rosa Parks left Maxwell Field on a bus, she was on a segregated vehicle.

Gandhi's Early Experiences in Natal

Mrs. Parks was determined to vote. In 1943 she made her first attempt to register and found the bureaucratic obstacles were formidable. The state would open the voting office at unannounced times or from 10–12 am, a time when most blacks were working, and employers certainly would not give them the time off to attempt to register to vote. Blacks who somehow made it to the designated offices faced officials who did their best to stop the would-be voters. The process for each applicant was deliberately slow. Applicants who did not own property were often demeaned; they were certainly forced to take a literacy test, usually with difficult questions about the Constitution. Mrs. Parks was told she failed. She tried again in 1943 and again she failed. As she later said, "They didn't have to give you a reason."

In April of 1945, the last year of World War II, she attempted to register once again and was given the literacy test. She said, "I made a copy of my answers to those twenty one questions." There were no Xerox copy machines then, but she copied her answers by hand: "I was going to keep that copy and use it to bring suit against the voter registration board." She passed; perhaps the officials saw her copying her answers and did not wish to face a law suit. There was another hurdle: the Poll Tax was $16.50, a large sum for poorly paid workers such as Rosa Parks.[3]

Mrs. Parks was fortunate in her struggle to vote; millions of other African Americans were told they failed the test, but most did not even make the attempt, knowing the officials were intent on refusal.

****

Gandhi had not voted previously in Natal and was therefore among the disenfranchised. He saw that he would need to extend his stay if he were to work effectively to remedy the many problems faced by Indians in Natal. He would not take funds for his public work, but he calculated it would take £300 a year for him to live on the scale of a barrister. Prosperous Indian merchants (mostly Muslims) agree to consulting fees for the income he needed and he would have time for the multiple activities needed to press for rights for his people. He told his supporters that his duties would mainly be "making you all work."[4] This argument was only partially true, for organizing volunteers took much time, and Gandhi with his legal knowledge and his skills in English and in clear writing had to be the one producing documents, petitions, letters, and interviews.

With his economic needs taken care of he rented a large home in an up-scale neighborhood on the beach—a house called Beach Grove Villa. Mr. Harry Escombe, Attorney General of Natal and legal advisor for Dada Abdulla and Co was his next door neighbor. Beach Grove Villa was a two story semi-detached house with a drawing room, dining room with table and chairs for eight, and five bedrooms.[5] Gandhi needed clerks in his newly established and busy law office, and these clerks often lived with him.

After long hours in his office, he was at his best at night meals with his clerks and visitors. He was jovial, informed, interested in the ideas of those around him, including those of his visitors. He continued to dress in Western fashion and daily walked to and from his office, the very picture of a successful attorney,

Gandhi applied for admission as an advocate to the Supreme Court of Natal, his petition being presented by Mr. Escombe. The Law Society objected, but after some delays he was enrolled: his credentials from the Inner Temple were difficult to overlook or deny, though the Law Society in a delaying move had objected that his English certificate was a copy, not the original. The main objection was that he was colored. The Chief Justice declared: "The law makes no distinction between white and coloured people," and Gandhi took the oath.

The Chief Justice then said, "You must now take off your turban, Mr. Gandhi. You must submit to the rules of the Court with regard to the dress to be worn by practising barristers."[6] Gandhi had refused such a request only a year previously, but he agreed this time, for he believed he should reserve his strength for larger battles. Most of the Natal newspapers supported Gandhi's efforts to appear before the Supreme Court.

Gandhi's Early Experiences in Natal

****

From slavery time in the South until the middle of the 1950s African American professionals such as attorneys and physicians were unable to enroll in the major professional societies which were white only. African Americans were denied entrance into the professional schools and universities in the former Confederate states. Dr. Furman Jeremiah Shadd, an African American, received his medical degree from Howard University in 1881, joined the faculty there and was appointed a full professor in 1891. He was a highly regarded physician, but when he applied to the local American Medical Association for membership he was denied because of his race.[7]

During the Civil War, a few men of color who were physicians were able to serve in the Union Army as doctors. Dr. A. T. Augusta, born a free black in Norfolk, Virginia, studied medicine in Toronto and received his medical degree in 1856. He then practiced in Toronto until the war began. He travelled to Washington, D. C. to take the examination necessary for appointment to the Union Medical corps. He was initially rejected because of his African descent and because he was a British subject. He replied that he expected to serve in a black regiment and that although his medical degree was from a Canadian school, he was an American citizen. His explanation was accepted but he needed to pass an oral examination on his medical knowledge and skills given by Dr. Cronyn. Later, Surgeon General Hammond asked, "I say Cronyn how did you come to let that nigger pass?" Dr. Cronyn replied, "The fact is, general, that the nigger knew more than I did and I could not help myself."[8]

Gandhi and Dr. Augusta were in much the same positions. They had the necessary credentials. The Union Army needed Dr. Augusta, and the Chief Justice of the Natal Supreme Court recognized that the law was color blind, even though most of the citizens of Natal were not.

Gandhi suggested the formation of the Natal Indian Congress in 1894, with plans to agitate for Indian rights. Annual subscription was, at a minimum, £3, which meant the membership was almost entirely drawn from Indian merchants. Gandhi tried to enlarge the base by establishing the Indian Educational Association for young people, appealing especially to the educated colonial-born Indians. It was akin to a debating society, with regular meetings, papers read and discussed, and there were efforts to bring these young people into contact with Indian merchants.[9]

The Natal Indian Congress had one needed component: propaganda. Gandhi wanted to make Europeans in South Africa, British subjects in the home country, and the people aware of conditions faced by Indians in Natal. He began by putting together detailed pamphlets about Indian hardships. He was using some first-hand knowledge, court records, newspaper accounts, and newspaper articles.

An incident with a Tamil indentured laborer named Balasundaram brought Gandhi directly into accounts of mistreatments of men of color who worked in the fields of Natal. The crying Tamil arrived in Gandhi's office wearing tattered clothes, his two front teeth broken, his mouth bleeding, and his turban in hand as a sign of respect. Gandhi's clerk, a Tamil Christian, translated for the two men. The injured man had been beaten by a well-known European. Gandhi took Balasundaram to a European physician who wrote a certificate about the injuries suffered by the Tamil. Gandhi then took the Tamil to the magistrate and submitted the physician's document. The angry magistrate summonsed the employer.

Gandhi did not want to get the European punished, but he did desire to help the suffering Tamil. Gandhi told the European that he did not wish to proceed against him, but he wanted Belasundaram transferred to another employer. Gandhi then found another employer for his client.[10]

Indentured laborers in the colony learned of Gandhi's efforts and came to him with their problems. He worked with them and gave them hope that their plights would be addressed. Gandhi's public work was taking on a new dimension as he began to serve the downtrodden Indians who had few rights.

****

Gandhi's Early Experiences in Natal

During slavery in the former Confederate states and then well into the 1950s, law officials took almost no interest in white assaults on people of color. A.T. Jones, a slave born in Kentucky, escaped to Canada and wrote about his life in bondage: "There was a near neighbor of ours, named Duncan, who whipped a slave to death. I knew about it myself; it was only half a mile from our place. No notice at all was taken of it. I suppose it was scarcely his intention to kill the man because it was the only man he had, but he got into a passion. The man went out against his orders."[11]

In the South after Reconstruction, whites who beat or lynched African Americans were almost never brought to justice. Many attorneys were afraid to take African Americans as clients, even when it was clear that the charges against the person of color were weak or manufactured. White lawyers with a black clientele were routinely labeled "nigger lovers." Gandhi was an educated attorney, and he was a gentleman, but he began to represent semi-slaves in South Africa. Whites could not damage him economically because his income came from successful Indian businessmen.

****

Gandhi continued to study world religions as he settled into life in Durbin. He read a translation of the *Upanishads*, *The Sayings of Zarathustra*, Washington Irving's *Life of Mahomet and His Successors*, and Thomas Carlyle on the Prophet. He continued to be interested in Christianity, especially religious books by Tolstoy. He commented on his study of various religious faiths, they "stimulated my self-introspection and fostered in me the habit of putting into practice whatever appealed to me in my studies."[12]

In the latter two years of Gandhi's first stay in South Africa—that is 1895 and 1896—he wrote that he was "absorbed in the service of the community" and "the reason behind it was my desire for self-realization." He made "the religion of service" his own.[13] Before he left for a six month stay in India in 1896, he had decided that his service to Indians in South Africa was only temporary, and sometime in the future work in his homeland was his destiny.

Gandhi lived in a whirlwind of activity during the day at his law office, but at night he had a salon in his dining room, with his clerks and visitors in attendance. He employed a cook and undoubtedly other servants to keep his household orderly. He felt the need of a major domo and a companion since his wife and two children remained in India. Mrs. Gandhi could undoubtedly have managed the household, but Gandhi sent for Sheikh Mehtab, probably in 1894. Mehtab was never one to keep his activities with Gandhi quiet, and it is most likely the extended Gandhi family in Rajkot soon learned that this man who had brought such tribulation to Gandhi and his wife was to take up life at Beach Grove Villa. Mrs. Gandhi had long recognized the duplicitous nature of Mehtab and must have been angered.

Mehtab arrived in Durban, and Gandhi in his *Autobiography* refers to him "as companion and help," without giving details. He does not use Mehtab's name. Mehtab's possessiveness had not changed. Early in Mehtab's stay in Durban, Gandhi reported, he "became jealous of an office clerk who was staying with me, and wove such a tangled web that I suspected the clerk." Were the suspicions financial? Personal? Sexual? Gandhi gives no details. When Gandhi and Mehtab were in high school, Mehtab had destroyed Gandhi's friendship with a fellow student and had spread lies about Mrs. Gandhi, making Gandhi more dependent on him. Gandhi seems to have suffered from amnesia. The falsely accused clerk left Gandhi's employ and moved out of Beach Grove Villa. Gandhi was a true believer in the clerk's guilt. Mehtab was a Svengali, and the clerk was fortunate to leave this hot-house environment controlled by an evil and controlling friend of a lawyer bedazzled by a friend from high school days.

Gandhi's regular cook had to go away for a few days, and a temporary cook was employed. Unfortunately, he was not a satisfactory cook, but he was an observant man, and he was not afraid to tell his employer about the irregularities he was observing.

Normally, Gandhi went home at 1 p.m. for lunch. One day at 12 noon, the cook arrived at Gandhi's office, panting from his quick walk.

Gandhi's Early Experiences in Natal

"Please come home at once. There is a surprise for you."

"Now, what is this? You must tell me what it is. How can I leave the office at this hour to go and see it?"

"You will regret it, if you don't come. That is all I can say."

Gandhi went home, accompanied by his clerk, Vincent Lawrence, and the cook.

The cook took Gandhi upstairs and stopped at Mehtab's room and said, "Open the door and see for yourself."

Gandhi knocked. No response.

He knocked heavily.

The door was opened, and Gandhi saw a prostitute inside. He told her to leave and not return.

To Mehtab, Gandhi said, "From this moment I cease to have anything to do with you. I have been thoroughly deceived and have made a fool of myself. That is how you have requited my trust in you."

Mehtab then threatened to expose Gandhi, but the *Autobiography* gives no details. Some writers who have commented on this incident see Mehtab as blustering at this point, but he was Gandhi's closest friend who had undoubtedly talked to Gandhi about his secret fears, his dreams, his fantasies, his hidden life. When the two boys were in high school, Mehtab took Gandhi to a prostitute (Gandhi left before having sex), but it was clear from that incident that Mehtab used prostitutes himself. Gandhi had probably told Mehtab about his near fall into an assignation with a prostitute in England. Would Mehtab have revealed his tangled emotional entanglement with Gandhi over a period of many years? We don't know; it may not have been bluster.

Mehtab argued even more, and Gandhi called to Vincent Lawrence, standing downstairs, to go to the Superintendent of Police to report that a man in the house had behaved improperly and would not leave. He asked for police help. At that point, Mehtab saw that his friend meant to take action against him, apologized, and agreed to leave.[14]

Writing in his *Autobiography*, Gandhi reflected on the scene: "The incident came as a timely warning in my life. Only now could I see clearly how thoroughly I had been beguiled by this evil genius. In harbouring him I had chosen a bad means for a good end. I had known that the companion was a bad character, and yet I believed in his faithfulness to me. In the attempt to reform him I was near ruining myself. I had disregarded the warnings of kind friends. Infatuation had completely blinded me."[15]

Gandhi praised the cook for having the courage to report what others in the household knew, for the prostitute had been there before, but they were afraid to speak.

Having recognized his folly in trusting Mehtab, Gandhi tried to make amends to the clerk slandered by Mehtab. Gandhi apologized, but the clerk was not satisfied. What is particularly interesting in this episode of Gandhi's attempt to make this matter right with the clerk is that it is not clear that Gandhi had never stopped believing stories Mehtab told about Mrs. Gandhi. This would suggest that Gandhi had not apologized to her for his distrust. Mehtab did sever all relations with Gandhi, who stayed in South Africa and in later years supported the Gandhi movement.

Gandhi's law practice was successful, and he was vigorously presenting the Indian cause in South Africa, but his personal life was in shambles. He was now alienated from his closest friend and was living without his wife and children. In 1896 he decided to take a six month leave to go to India to educate public opinion about Indian conditions in the South African colonies and to bring his wife and children to Durban to live with him.[16]

NOTES

1. Gandhi, *Autobiography*, pp. 176–80.
2. Ibid., pp. 193–96.
3. Douglas Brinkley, *Rosa Parks*, pp. 41–43; 55–60.
4. Gandhi, *Autobiography*, pp. 179–81.
5. Martin Green, *Gandhi*, pp. 176–77.
6. Gandhi, *Autobiography*, pp. 181–83.
7. George Hendrick and Willene Hendrick, *Black Refugees in Canada*, pp. 67–68.
8. Ibid., pp. 107–8.
9. Gandhi, *Autobiography*, pp. 185–89.
10. Ibid., pp. 190–92.
11. John W. Blassingame, *Slave Testimony*, pp. 430–31.
12. Gandhi, *Autobiography*, p. 198.
13. Ibid., p. 197.
14. Ibid., pp. 201–04. .
15. Ibid., p. 203.
16. Ibid., p. 205.

CHAPTER V

GANDHI AND THE ULTIMATE IN RACISM

LYNCHING

A group of prominent men in the India community gave Gandhi £75 for travel, printing costs, and other expenses during his six months of leave in India. Gandhi kept a careful account of his daily expenses charged to that account, and those expenses are printed in *The Collected Works of Mahatma Gandhi,* II: 139–153. Wanting to learn the languages of his countrymen, he purchased books in Tamil, Hindi, Urdu, and Bengali. He also bought several books on local laws in India to gather information on the franchise and on more representative government India.

During the 24 day trip to Calcutta, Gandhi studied Urdu, in order to have closer contacts with Muslims and Tamil, to be closer in touch with Indians from Madras. This early in his career, Gandhi had learned that the fight in South Africa "was for the poor," and he wished to communicate with them by learning their languages as best he could.[1]

Gandhi also had extensive spiritual discussion with the captain of the ship he was on, the S.S. *Pongola*. The captain was a member of the Plymouth Brethren, a fundamentalist religious group. According to

Gandhi, the captain believed "Let all, men, women and children,...have faith in Jesus and his sacrifice and their sins were sure to be redeemed." And religion "that imposed any moral restrictions was to him no good." Gandhi argued that "religion and morality were synonymous," and the two men could not come to an agreement.[2]

Gandhi landed in Calcutta, and the next day he left by train for the long trip to Bombay. The train stooped for 45 minutes in Allahabad, and he decided to spend the time taking a drive through the city and stopping at the chemist's shop to purchase some medicine. The chemist was slow, and Gandhi missed the train. The Station Master had requested that Gandhi's luggage be removed before the departure. Gandhi had a day before the next train, and he called on Mr. Chesney, Jr., editor of *The Pioneer*. That newspaper, Gandhi believed, was opposed to Indian aspirations. Chesney heard Gandhi discuss the Indian problem and promised to notice in the paper anything Gandhi wrote about the matter, but he said he could not promise to endorse the Indian demands, "inasmuch as he was bound to understand and give due weight to the viewpoint of the Colonials as well."[3] Gandhi responded: "It is enough that you should study the question and discuss it in your paper. I ask and desire nothing but the barest justice that is due to us."[4] Gandhi had a way of disarming his opponents by asking only for fair play.

This hastily arranged interview in a newspaper office began a series of incidents which concluded some months later with Gandhi's serious beating, followed later that same day by an attempt to lynch him.

Gandhi went on to Bombay, but did not stay there, as he had done when he returned from London. Instead, he went directly to Rajkot where he was reunited with his wife and two sons. Almost immediately he set out to write *The Grievances of the British Indians in South Africa. An Appeal to the Indian Public*, now known as the "Green Pamphlet" because of the color of the cover. The writing took about a month, and the first printing of 5,000 copies soon appeared. The pamphlet is closely argued, clearly written, and filled with specific details about the treatment of Indians in

Gandhi and the Ultimate in Racism

the four colonies which were eventually united into the Union of South Africa. Gandhi was not afraid to discuss the deep-seated hatred of Indians throughout the colonies.

Gandhi set the stage for Indian grievances by giving some uncontested facts. Natal, where most of the Indians lived, had an African population of about 40,000, a European population of approximately 50,000, an Indian population of about 51,000, with about 16,000 indentured (mostly Hindu). About 30,000 Indians had once been indentured but had served their term and had remained in Natal. About 5,000 (mostly Muslim) belonged to the trading community.

Indians were called "coolies," and were degraded as "bearers of wood and drawers of water." Railroad officials generally treated Indians as beasts. Hotels and public baths were closed to Indians.[5] The litany of injustices was long and similar to many problems faced by people of color in the segregated South in 1896.

Gandhi then turned to showing that the feeling of hatred towards Indians "has been crystallized into legislation."[6] In Southern states in the United States, legislation taking away rights of people of color advanced more quickly after the "separate but equal" decision in *Plessy v. Ferguson*, the same year as Gandhi's Green Pamphlet. Indians and Africans could not be out at night without having a pass.

The Natal government was intent on forcing Indians to return to India. The heavy taxes would force most Indians to leave. The government wanted to disenfranchise Indians, for it was feared that Indians would swamp Europeans and rule South Africa.[7] These same fears were prevalent in the South in 1896, as there was a rolling tide of disenfranchisement of African Americans.

As the *Natal Mercury* noted on March 5, 1896, "the superior race [European] will always hold the reins of Government."[8]

Turning to the Cape Colony, Gandhi wrote that "the Mayoral Congress has passed a resolution signifying its desire for legislation prohibiting the influx of Asiatics in that Colony...." The Cape Legislature gave the East London Municipality "the power to make bye-laws compelling natives and Indians to remove to and reside in certain locations and prohibiting them from walking on foot-paths." Gandhi also notes that Indian traders were "unceremoniously refused licenses to trade.: Indian traders posed an economic threat to European businesses.[9]

****

Similarly, Wilson Ruffin Abbott, born a free black in Richmond Virginia in 1801, was forced from his business in Mobile. Abbott early in life was a steward on a Mississippi riverboat and was injured when a stack of wood fell on him. He was nursed back to health by a maid, Ellen Toyer, who taught him to read and write. He was talented in mathematics and in business. In the 1830s he and Ellen Toyer, now his wife, opened a successful grocery in Mobile, Alabama. The city council, clearly working for the interests of white businesses, passed an ordinance that required all free blacks to post a bond which had been signed by two white men and to wear badges certifying that they were bonded. Abbott refused, and he then received an anonymous letter sayjng his store was going to be destroyed as well as warning him and his family to leave Mobile immediately. Abbott understood that he had to take the contents of that letter seriously; he put his wife and children on a ship going to New Orleans. He removed all his money from the bank and departed for New Orleans the next day. His store was then looted, a complete loss. The Abbotts moved to New York, then Canada, where he prospered. The white businessmen no longer had Abbott as a competitor.

The Cape Colony restrictions kept Indian businesses from operating. In fact, in East Griqualand, one or two licenses had already been issued, but those businesses were to be closed.[10]

****

The Transvaal, a non-English state, was controlled by Boers. Johannesburg was a boom town, with gold and diamond mines, immense wealth and grinding poverty. Indians could not take out mining licenses and were not allowed to sell or to own gold. Once again, Indians were feared as competitors, end Europeans controlled the mines.[11]

The Orange Free State, another Boer-controlled colony, had effectively driven out Indians from its borders. Gandhi spoke directly: "The law, which is entitled 'the law to prevent the inrush of Asiatic coloured persons,' prevents any Indian from remaining in the Orange Free State for more than 2 months, unless he gets the permission from the President of the Republic, who cannot consider the application to reside before thirty days have elapsed after the presentation of the petition and other ceremonies have been performed. He can, however, on no account, hold fixed property in the State or carry on any mercantile or farming business."[12]

****

A similar denial of basic rights was present in the late nineteenth and early twentieth century in the United States—"Sundown Towns." These towns were largely in the midwest, though they could occasionally be found in isolated southern areas; they enforced laws or tradition which allowed no African American to spend the night. African Americans were effectively banished, as they were in the Orange Free State.[13]

****

Gandhi demonstrated with example after example that government officials in the South African colonies did not act decisively to protect Indians. Gandhi, though, still thought of himself as a faithful subject of Empress Victoria. He believed that "pressure from the Home Government can bring about a healthy change in the Indian policy of the Colonies, and that, even in the worst places, British love of justice and fair play can be roused."[14] In 1896 he could not imagine what pressures would be needed to bring about change.

Gandhi concluded the pamphlet by stating he was detailing Indian grievances in order "to enlist the very active sympathy of all the public bodies in India." The Green Pamphlet did receive attention; the first printing of 5,000 copies sold out, and a second printing of 4,000 was needed. Gandhi gave several speeches on Indian grievances in cities across the country. His examples were often shocking; in an address given in Madras he noted it was part of public opinion in elements of South Africa that we "breed like rabbits." A gentleman at a meeting in Durban said that he "was sorry we could not be shot like them."[15]

In an address given in Bombay, Gandhi mentioned a growing concern of his, since he had two sons and the son of his widowed sister who were being taken to Durban. He does not make this issue personal in the speech, however. He said, "The High Schools are not open to the Indians. A fortnight before I left Natal, an Indian student applied for admission to the Durban High School and his application was rejected. Even the primary schools are not quite open to the Indians. An Indian missionary schoolmaster was driven out of an English Church in Verulam, a small village in Natal."[16]

****

The 1954 decision of the Supreme Court in *Brown v. Board of Education of Topeka, Kansas*, led to the end of Jim Crow Laws, but the desegregation of schools proved difficult. In 1957 Governor Orville Faubus posted 270 National Guardsmen around Central High School in Little Rock, Arkansas, in an attempt to keep nine black students from entering. A district court ordered Faubus to admit the students, and he removed the guard, allowing angry crowds to vilify and endanger the nine students. President Eisenhower then sent paratroopers and put the state's national guardsmen under federal authority to open the school to blacks.[17] While this example is more violent than the educational situation faced by Indians in South Africa, Gandhi was certainly faced with the major issue of education for his sons. As a prominent barrister, he might have found a school which would accept his sons and nephew, but would they be welcomed? Harassed? Gandhi was aware that the boys would be subjected to curses and to isolation.

****

Gandhi naively believed that color prejudice in South Africa was temporary and "quite contrary to British traditions," forgetting the long and profitable slave trade and the color prejudice indulged in by the British throughout the British Empire. Gandhi was a loyal subject. In Rajkot he was a member of the committee established for the celebration of Empress Victoria's Diamond Jubilee. He even taught the National Anthem to the children.

Once the Green pamphlet was printed, Gandhi was faced with the problem of mailing out thousands of copies. Instead of hiring help to do the addressing, Gandhi gathered children in the neighborhood to do this secretarial work. Once the job was finished he gave them used postage stamps he had been collecting.

Gandhi wanted to make himself known, and he wanted to meet important intellectual, religious, and political leaders while he was in India. He also wanted to pass on the Green Pamphlet to them. In the speeches he gave in various parts of the country he summarized the contents of that pamphlet.

Gandhi probably gave the Green Pamphlet to his Jain friend, Rajchandra, with whom he had previously corresponded about religious matters, but in their conversation in India he heard this brilliant man discuss *brahmachari*—that is chastity—even for those who were married.[18] Gandhi was not ready to explore that subject and he was to father two more sons. Rajchandra's praise of chastity remained with him.

The most important political and intellectual figure Gandhi met was Gopal Krishna Gokhale, Professor of Mathematics, English, and Political Economy at Fergusson College. Gokhale advised Gandhi on what people to meet and looked over his speech. He was a moderate in political matters and deeply influenced Gandhi's approach to political matters.[19] Gandhi also met Bal Gangadhar Tilak, scholar and writer whose extremist views were radically different from Gokhale's. Gandhi resisted being influenced by Tilak.[20]

When Gandhi was in India he showed particular interest in public health and in nursing. Because of an outbreak of plague in Bombay, there was fear that it would spread to Rajkot, where he was staying. Gandhi felt he could serve the sanitation department and offered his services to the State. He was accepted and appointed to a committee investigating the matter. The cleaning of latrines was believed to necessary to stop the plague, but the upper classes generally opposed the suggestions of the committee. The committee members also visited the homes of untouchables and most often found their homes clean.[21] This early in his life, Gandhi had not thought through the problems of untouchables in Indian society, but in his sanitation work in Rajkot he saw a side of the lives of untouchables new to him.

During a stay in Bombay, Gandhi visited his sister and found her husband was seriously ill. His sister was unable to nurse her husband, and Gandhi removed him to Rajkot and personally supervised his care, staying with him night and day, just as he had nursed his father many years before. The patient died,[22] but nursing and medicine—natural cures, water cures—were to become passions of his during the next years.

Gandhi's stay in India had been successful; he had reconnected with his wife and children, had written and distributed the "Green Pamphlet," had met many leaders including intellectuals, attorneys, religious thinkers, and had made himself known in many areas of the vast country.

In the meantime, the Green Pamphlet was creating a controversy, but Gandhi was unaware of the dangers he faced. Mr. Chesney's *Pioneer* did publish a notice of the Green Pamphlet, and on September 14, 1896 a summary was telegraphed by Reuters to London. Reuters then cabled a two sentence summary of the summary to Natal: "A pamphlet published in India declares that the Indians in Natal are robbed and assaulted and

Gandhi and the Ultimate in Racism 77

treated like beasts, and are unable to obtain address. The *Times of India* advocates an inquiry into these allegations."[23] Gandhi had thought the pamphlet was "a subdued picture,"[24] of Indian problems in South Africa, but he had used many explosive illustrations of the injustices. Gandhi correctly pointed out that the Reuters cable "was a miniature, but exaggerated, edition of the picture I had drawn...and it was not in my words."[25] The two sentence summary created violent reaction in Durban and led to two attempts on Gandhi's life, but Gandhi was unaware of events in Natal.

The Reuters miniature story about the Green Pamphlet brought about the formation of various protest groups. Europeans met on September 18, 1896, in Mauritzburg to found a European Protective Association. About thirty persons attended the meeting which went on record as urging the Natal Parliament to institute rules and regulations forcing Indians to leave the Colony as soon as their indenture had been served and to limit the number of Indians allowed into the Colony.[26]

A similar organization, the Colonial Patriotic Union, was formed in Durban on November 26, 1896. The Union wanted to prevent the further immigration of free Asiatic races into the Colony. Again, the organization demanded that indentured laborers return to India at the end of their indentures. The government was in sympathy with the white supremacy organizations.[27]

Two newspapers showed some sympathy for Gandhi and his account of discrimination against Indians in Natal. The Natal *Mercury* on September 18, 1896, defended Gandhi's rights to work on behalf of his fellow Indians and asserted that the two sentence Reuters report was an exaggeration. The Natal *Advertiser* that same day agreed that the Reuters telegraphed story did not accurately reflect the contents of the Green Pamphlet and concluded that it was "easy to sympathise" with Gandhi and his compatriots.[28]

On November 12, 1896, Gandhi received a cable from Dada Abdulla, Durban, requesting him to return to Natal, for the *Volksraad* (National

Legislative Assembly in the Transvaal) and the Orange Free State had now recommended that Indians should be forced to live in locations, that is, ghettos.[29] Gandhi made plans to leave for Durban, and with his family and his nephew sailed on November 30, 1896 on the *S. S. Courland*, owned by Dada Abdulla. Dada Abdulla provided free passage for the family.

Gandhi was forced to think about the appearance of his family; he did not ask his wife to participate in these decisions, for she was virtually unlettered and was not aware of Western ways. Even so, she might have had valuable suggestions, but the autocratic Gandhi did not consult with her. He decided that Parsis were the most civilized people in India; therefore, when European style was unsuitable, he wanted to adopt Parsi style. Mrs. Gandhi wore a Parsi *sari*. Gandhi does not mention this, but she was not adorned with jewelry; it had been sold to help pay for his three years of study in London. The two Gandhi sons and nephew wore the Parsi coat and trousers. All had to wear shoes and stockings, and Mrs. Gandhi and the children had trouble getting used to them: the shoes hurt their feet and the stockings smelled of perspiration. There were protests, but Gandhi was the one with authority. Gandhi, himself, continued to dress as an English gentleman. He also insisted that the entire family use knives and forks when eating.[30] The photographs of Mrs. Gandhi during her early years in South Africa show her to be a beautiful woman, but she appears withdrawn, suffering from the demanding ways of a typical Indian husband.

At the same time the *Courland* departed, the *Naderi* also left; the agent for that ship was Dada Abdulla and Co. Together the two ships carried about 800 Indians, about half of whom were planning to settle in the Transvaal, an unwelcoming haven.

Four days before the *Courland* was to arrive in Durban, a violent gale began to rock the ship. The passengers became alarmed. Gandhi wrote in his *Autobiography* that they "became one in the face of the common danger. They forgot their differences and began to think of the one and only God—Musalmans, Hindus, Christians and all." The captain joined the passengers in prayer. The fear of death was palpable. After twenty

Gandhi and the Ultimate in Racism

four hours, the storm was over, and God disappeared from the lips of the passengers. During the storm itself, Gandhi, a good sailor, moved among the frightened passengers giving aid and comfort to the frightened passengers.[31] Gandhi was more at ease and more understanding and empathetic with strangers than he was with his wife and children, with whom he was often stern and unbending.

The storm at sea was nothing in comparison to the storm brewing in Durban. On December 18, 1896, the *Courland* and *Naderi* reached Durban, but they were not allowed to land passengers because there had been outbreaks of the bubonic plague in Bombay before the ships departed there. At first a five day period of quarantine was put in place

Gandhi continued to assist passengers, helping to organize games for entertainment. On Christmas Day, at a dinner arranged by the captain, Gandhi gave a serious speech, defending himself from the charges that he condemned Natal whites while he was in India. He spoke forcefully denying that he was responsible for bringing two shiploads of Indians to South Africa or of condemning South African whites when he was in India. He deplored Western civilization "of which the Natal whites were the fruit and which they represented and championed."[32]

Afterwards, Gandhi had extended conversations with Captain Milne and officers on the ship, and he believed it was the captain who asked him, referring to the threats against Gandhi in the mass meetings in Durban: "Supposing the whites carry out their threats, how will you stand by your principle of non-violence?"

Gandhi responded: "I hope God will give me the courage and the sense to forgive them, and to refrain from bringing them to court. I have no anger against them. I am only sorry for their ignorance and their narrowness. I know that they sincerely believe that what they are doing is right and proper. I have no reason, therefore, to be angry with them."[33]

The tensions in Durban rose while the ships were under quarantine, and the passengers on the *Courland* and *Naderi* were being harassed. Although there was no indication of plague on the two ships, they were ordered to be fumigated. The officials later ordered that the bedclothes of the passengers should be burned, leaving suffering passengers. [34]

The European residents of Durban, who had formed a Demonstration Committee, were holding "monster meetings" about the Asian threat. Natal's Attorney General, Harry Escombe, a friend of Gandhi's, was a leading member of a protest group trying to keep the 800 Indians on two ships from entering Durban.[35] The leaders of the various protest movements wanted to pass strict anti-Asian laws similar to those already in place in Australia and New Zealand. The rhetoric was inflammatory, as these passages from speeches of the white supremacists show:

"Why don't you bring Gandhi ashore?"

"Get the tar and feathers ready."

Dr. MacKenzie, one of the leaders: "He was just as game as anybody to take a coolie by the neck and throw him overboard." (applause).

"The greatest service they could do him [Gandhi] would be to do him an injury."

"...Gandhi was very anxious to become a hero and a martyr to his cause."

"If he [Gandhi] lived amongst them, they would have an opportunity of spitting on him." (laughter and applause)

These sentences were manifestoes for mob rule.[36]

The Demonstration Committee called upon the European merchants to close their businesses in order for the owners and employees to take part in a demonstration at the harbor when the Indians—and especially Gandhi—debarked. The Demonstration Committee could then "be able to see who was on their side. Several merchants had already promised to do all they could, others they wanted to show in their true colours (cries of 'boycott them')."[37]

Gandhi and the Ultimate in Racism 81

Indians already living in Durban were peaceful all during this period of race hatred. On January 3, 1897, Gandhi, still on the *Courland*, was interviewed by a reporter for the Natal *Advertiser*. Gandhi defended the Green Pamphlet and pointed out that members of the Demonstration were "disloyal" to the British Empire. Gandhi still believed that the British government would protect all its subjects.

Harry Escombe, who had revealed his white supremacy views in supporting mob rule, now had a change in tactics. He wrote at 10:45 on January 13, 1897, that the two steamers would be allowed to unload their passengers at 12 noon that day. He then added: "The Government needs no reminder of its responsibility for the maintenance of order."[38]

Nevertheless, several thousand people had converged at the Point at the harbor. From railway men there were 900 to 1,000; from the Yacht Club, Rowing Club, and Point Club, 150; Carpenters and Joiners, 450; printers, 80; tailors and saddlers, 70; plasterers and bricklayers, 200; general public, 1,000; native section (probably Zulus) and undoubtedly paid demonstrators, 500.

The Africans described in the article were described as providing comic relief. The organizers appointed a native dwarf as the leader, and the little person marched before his African troops, "while they went through a number of exercises with their sticks, and danced and whooped." This diversion was supposedly to keep the natives out of trouble,[39] but causing trouble is why the organizers had arranged for them to be there.

Mr. Escombe addressed the mob, promising that Parliament could soon deal with the Asiatic problem and requested that the crowd be dispersed. The crowd did dwindle away, but not before calling out many insults and threats to Gandhi.

The passengers disembarked but Gandhi and his family remained on board. Mr. Escombe had sent word to the captain that the Europeans were enraged about Gandhi and suggested the Gandhis depart at dusk. Soon, Mr. Laughton, legal advisor for the firm of Dada Abdulla and Co. and

Gandhi's friend, approached the captain. He proposed that Mr. Escombe's advice be ignored. He then spoke to Gandhi: "If you not afraid, I suggest that Mrs. Gandhi and the children should drive to Mr. Rustomji's house, whilst you and I follow them on foot. I do not at all like the idea of your entering the city like a thief in the night. I do not think there is any fear of anyone hurting you. Everything is quiet now. The whites have all dispersed. But in any case you ought not to enter the city stealthily."

Gandhi agreed.

Laughton did not understand the dangers Gandhi faced.

Mrs. Gandhi and the children were driven to the home of Mr. Rustomji, a wealthy Parsi merchant, where they were to spend the night. Gandhi put on his turban and left with Mr. Laughton.

The two men left the ship and were ready to begin the two mile walk to the Rustomji home at about 4:30 on an overcast day. Normally, the walk would have taken about an hour. Some European boys saw them. Gandhi does not suggest this, but it is possible the protestors were paying idle boys to be on the lookout for the "coolie" barrister.

Gandhi had on a turban of a particular type, and the boys recognized him. They began to shout "Gandhi," "Gandhi," "thrash him," "surround him," and they came running and began to throw pebbles at the two men, one small, one large and powerful. A few adult Europeans joined the boys, and then the crowd grew. Mr. Laughton saw that the two of them needed to get away quickly and hailed a rickshaw. Gandhi was opposed to being pulled by another human being, but reluctantly he was willing to ride in a rickshaw if it meant he could escape the gathering mob. The adults and boys chasing the deadly Asian menace and his protector threatened the Zulu rickshaw puller: if he accepted these passengers, he would be beaten and his rickshaw destroyed.

"Kha," (no) was his response, and he fled, leaving the would-be passengers to continue by foot.

Gandhi and the Ultimate in Racism 83

With adults in the mob, pebbles became stones, and then whatever else that came to hand was thrown at Gandhi. His turban was knocked off, and then a burly man slapped his face and kicked him. Gandhi almost lost consciousness, but managed to hold on to the railings of a nearby house. When his fainting spell was over, he continued on his way, but he had given up hope of surviving this vicious attack.

He then saw coming the other way Mrs. Alexander, wife of the superintendent of the Durban police.

Gandhi knew her and her husband well. She was a brave lady; faced by a mob, she opened her umbrella to shield Gandhi and walked close beside him. The mob had a problem; they did not want to insult her or hurt her, but they kept aiming blows at Gandhi, but these were less painful than the ones he had previously received. In the meantime, an Indian boy, seeing the melee, had run to the police station to report the assault on Gandhi.

Superintendent Alexander sent constables to protect Gandhi; they surrounded him and took him to the police station. Alexander, having rescued Gandhi and Mrs. Alexander from a dangerous situation, offered Gandhi asylum in the police station, but Gandhi refused. He thanked Mr. and Mrs. Alexander for their help. He continued: "They are sure to quiet down when they realize their mistake." Gandhi said, "I have trust in their sense of fairness." Within a few hours, he was proven wrong. Escorted by the police, he reached Mr. Rustomji's home, where he was treated by Dr. Dadibarjor, doctor on the Courland. One of Gandhi's wounds was particularly painful, but he praised the efforts of the physician.[40]

****

A few decades earlier, specifically in 1843, Frederick Douglass had been attacked by a similar mob in Indiana. Douglass, a black man who had escaped from slavery, was in that state to speak at abolitionist rallies. With him were two white men, George Bradburn and Willlam White. At Pendleton, Indiana, the three abolitionists spent the night with a local physician Sometime during the night of September 14, they were informed "that a mob had threatened to come down from...a miserable, rum-drinking place, about six miles distant" to drive out the race-mixed abolitionists. More than likely the attackers drank corn whisky instead of rum. The attackers decided to study the problem before taking action. The next day, Douglass, a master orator, spoke at a Baptist church without interruption, but more men than usual were in attendance. Leaders of that church also were aware of the observing men and decided that the abolitionists could not use the church that afternoon, fearing it would be destroyed.

The three abolitionist speakers conducted their meeting from the steps of the church, but they were heckled by about thirty men. Before there were any blows struck, a storm blew in and caused the entire crowd to disperse. That evening, the town's citizens met and passed a resolution declaring the abolitionists should be allowed to speak.

William White, a recent Harvard graduate, wrote an account of this attack in Indiana for William Lloyd Garrison's Liberator. "The next morning being pleasant," White wrote, "we held our meeting in the woods, where seats and stands had been arranged." At the start of the meeting, White saw only about seven opposed to the abolitionists among the hundred men end thirty women present at the camp meeting-like affair. Bradburn spoke first, and as he attacked the institution of slavery, the mob began to gather; these country men were menacing, with sneers on their faces. At a signal, the mob walked out. Then there was a shout, and about thirty men, undoubtedly likkered-up, rushed two-by-two into the gathering, carrying with them rocks and rotten eggs. The leader wore a coon-skin cap. The audience started to essape. White urged them to remain seated but most of the men departed. "Surround them" the leader cried, and the three abolitionists were pelted with rocks and rotten eggs; they were stoical, for Garrison believed in nonviolence, and his followers embraced a nonviolent creed of not fighting back.

Stymied by the peaceful actions of the abolitionist speakers, the mob didn't quite know what to do; finally one asked why the abolitionists didn't

Gandhi and the Ultimate in Racism 85

take their message to the south. Bradburn called for that challenger to come forward and speak. White said that presentation was "a most ridiculous spectacle, interlading his speech with copious oaths, and ending off by saying he could not talk, but he could fight—that he had too much good blood in his veins to let us go on."

Then a man jumped on the platform and began to overturn a table and to push people around. Douglass thought White was in danger and forgetting Garrisonian nonviolence, grasped a piece of wood. There were cries from the mob: "kill the nigger, kill the damned nigger." The mob chased after Douglass, who had reason to fear for his life. White followed in an attempt to help his fellow-speaker. The mob caught up with Douglass, and one blow broke his right hand. White was able to deflect another blow of such violence it would have killed Douglass. White himself was hit in the head, blood flowing, and he lost some teeth. The two injured men were on the ground and the members of the mob rode away. A Quaker loaded them into the bed of his wagon, took them home, and his wife set to work cleaning and bandaging them.

The mob reaction against Douglass and his companions in Indiana and against Gandhi in Natal were similar in many ways. In both instances, elements wanted to kill men of color.[41]

****

As night approached, crowds of Europeans began to surround the Rustomji home, shouting "We must have Gandhi." Gandhi remarked that hooligans joined the Europeans, but there must have been hoodlums there already. The crowd was larger than the one in Indiana opposed to the abolitionists, but the aim was similar.

The mob of thousands sent word to Rustomji to give up Gandhi or the house and people inside would be burned to death. Rustomji did not give in to the demands. Fortunately, Superintendent Alexander had arrived with constables and detectives, and he and his men quietly joined the mob. He sent for a bench, stood on it, and while he was talking to the crowd, his men took possession of the front of the house, thereby assuring the house could not be entered by the mob. He also had one of his men disguise himself as an Indian trader by putting paint on his face and wearing Indian garb. The disguised policeman was able to enter the house with this message: "If you wish to save your friend, his guests and property, and your own family, I advise you to disguise yourself as an Indian constable, come out through Rustomji's *godown* [warehouse], steal through the crowd with my men and reach the Police Station. A carriage is awaiting you at the corner of the street. This is the only way in which I can save you and others. The crowd is so excited that I am not in a position to control it. If you are not prompt in following my directions, I am afraid the crowd will raze Rustomji's house to the ground and it is impossible for me to imagine how many lives will be lost and how much property destroyed."

Gandhi disguised himself as a constable, and with the police officer disguised as an Indian trader reached the Police Station. While the escape was being made, Mr. Alexander sang to the mob. Some were topical songs, but he also sang

Hang old Gandhi

On the sour apple tree.

Once Superintendent Alexander knew Gandhi was safe, he asked:

"What do you want?"

"We want Gandhi."

"What will you do with him?"

"We will burn him."

"What harm has he done to you?"

"He has vilified us in India and wants to flood Natal with Indians."

"What if he does not come out?"

Gandhi and the Ultimate in Racism

"We will then burn this house."

"His wife and children are also there. There are other men and women besides. Would you not be ashamed of burning women and children?"

"The responsibility for that will rest with you. What can we do when you make us helpless in the matter? We do not wish to hurt anyone else. It would be enough if you hand over Gandhi to us. If you do not surrender the culprit, and if others are injured in our endeavour to capture him, would it be fair on your part to blame us?"

The Superintendent then smiled and told the crowd that Gandhi had escaped and was already in a safe place. Gandhi reported that the mob then laughed, for he had tricked the mob. The crowd cried out: "It is a lie, it is a lie."

Mr. Alexander then had a proposal: The crowd would appoint a committee of three or four who would be allowed to enter the Rustomji home to search for Gandhi. If he were not found, the crowd would go peacefully to their homes.

Superintendent Alexander continued: "You got excited today and did not obey the police. That reflects discredit on you, not on the police. The police therefore played a trick with you; it removed your prey from your midst and you have lost the game. You will certainly not blame the police for this. The police, whom you yourselves have appointed, have simply done their duty."

The search committee reported that Gandhi was not to be found, and the disappointed crowd dispersed.[42]

****

After the Civil War was over, blacks began to be appointed to government positions, especially during Reconstruction. Later, President Harrison's postmaster general appointed thousands of blacks to positions in the post office. President McKinley continued, and many of these appointments were in the south, enraging the local whites.

Frazier B. Baker, then a forty year old, black teacher, a Republican, was named postmaster of Lake City, South Carolina in the fall of 1897. The white members of the community began efforts to get him out of office. They tried taking their mail to a nearby town and boycotting the Lake City Post office. Then they circulated a letter, sent to a minor official on the staff of the Postmaster General in Washington, urging Baker's removal because he was lazy and spoke impolitely to women of the town.

That December 1897 and also in January 1898, shots were fired at Baker and his assistant, who were not injured. Then in January the post office was destroyed by fire. Baker did not resign. He moved the post office to the living room of his home on the outskirts of town, infuriating whites of the area.

On the night of February 22, 1898, a mob of about three hundred completely surrounded Baker home, which contained a federal post office, set it on fire, and shot at those who began to flee. Baker was the first to die. Mrs. Baker and three children were shot, but survived as they fled. Mrs. Baker was carrying a baby, and the child was shot in the head and died.

Most white citizens did not deplore these lynchings and attempted murders. During investigations, the local citizens reported they saw nothing, knew nothing. How could anyone be tried and convicted? Members of the mob were certain to be on the jury.

There was outrage in the black community about this lynching, and the activist Ida Wells-Barnett went to Washington D.C. with several legislators to present their concerns to President McKinley, who told them that federal probe of the case was under way. In June of 1898, several men were arrested; some were acquitted and others freed because of hung juries. A federal Judge concerned with the cases wept, as a newspaper reported, "in sorrow for the shame which lynchers have brought upon his beloved state."[43]

****

Gandhi and the Ultimate in Racism

Gandhi's interview with a Durban newspaper took place on January 13, 1897, before he left the *Courland*. He set the record straight about his activities in India and about the contents of the Green Pamphlet, and his full account did help the Indian cause. Even many Europeans felt the mob action had been a mistake. Notice of the attempted lynching reached London, and Mr. Joseph Chamberlain, Secretary of State for the Colonies, sent a cable to the Natal government requesting the attackers be prosecuted and to see that justice was done.

Mr. Escombe, Attorney General in Natal, Gandhi's friend, one who early on urged the mob to action, called to express his regret.

Escombe said, "I can assure you that I did not at all intend that you or any other member of your community should be injured." He then tried to place the blame on Gandhi for not following his advice to leave the ship at dusk. Shifting his argument, he didn't wish to blame Gandhi for leaving when he did. He then announced that he wanted the offenders charged. "Can you identify any of your assailants?"

Gandhi responded that he might be able to identify one or two of them, but he did not plan to prosecute those who assailed him. He did not blame them for their actions: "Excited crowds have always tried to deal out justice in that manner."

Then Gandhi spoke truth to power: "If anyone is to blame it is the Committee of Europeans, you yourself and therefore the Government of Natal."

Mr. Escombe seems not to have heard and understood what Gandhi was saying to him. Instead, he was pleased that Gandhi was not prosecuting, for it would have been awkward for the government. He then asked Gandhi to write a note about the decision. Gandhi responded that he was making a religious decision and that he took "all responsibility" on his own shoulders. He immediately wrote out the note.[44]

****

The protest group led by Dr. Martin Luther King, Jr., had its own chance to speak truth to power on January 30, 1956. Rosa Parks had been arrested on December 1, 1955 for disobeying the segregation laws concerning seating on buses, and African Americans began a boycott of Montgomery, Alabama, city buses on December 5, 1955. City officials and the local police were segregationists and opposed the boycott. Blacks were harassed, and Dr. King began receiving anonymous death threats, such as, "Nigger if you aren't out of this town in three days we gonna blow your brains out and blow up your house."[45] Dr. King was frightened for himself, his wife, and infant daughter, but he continued his round of meetings supporting the boycott activities.

On the night of January 30, 1956, Dr. King was attending a mass meeting at the First Baptist Church, when a bomb exploded on the porch of the King home. People in the neighborhood began to gather, and Dr. King, on the platform was aware that something was wrong since ushers and others at the church were scurrying around. Finally Dr. King asked some trusted friends what the problem was, and he was told that his house had been bombed. His friends did not know the fate of Mrs. King and the baby. Before Dr. King left the church, he asked those in the audience to go home and to be nonviolent. Dr. King was already a believer in Gandhi's nonviolent methods.

Dr. King was driven home, and he found several hundred angry people around it. There was an air of violence in the air, and the police were treating members of the crowd in a rough manner. One black man, being hassled by a policeman, said, "I ain't gonna move nowhere. That's the trouble now, you white folks is always pushin' us around. Now you got your 38 and I got mine, so let's battle it out."[46] Inside, Dr. King found his wife and daughter safe. The mayor of Montgomery, W. A. Gayle, the police commissioner Clyde Sellers, and several reporters were standing in the dining room. Mayor Gayle and Police Commissioner Sellers expressed regret that "this unfortunate incident has taken place in our city." C. T. Smiley, chairman of the trustees of Dr. King's church, replied, "You may express your regrets, but you must face the fact that your public statements created the atmosphere for this bombing." The mayor and police commissioner, who had put in place a "get tough" policy against the boycott and the leaders, did not respond.

Dr. King then walked onto the blasted porch, the smell of dynamite still in the air. He told the angry crowd that his family was safe and asked them to go home and to act nonviolently: "We must meet hate with love."

The police commissioner then attempted to speak and was booed. Dr. King reminded this would-be mob to listen, and the commissioner offered a reward for those reporting the offenders.[47]

Dr. King's friend spoke truth to powerful segregationists and Dr. King steered an angry mob from near violence to a peaceful return to their own homes. A policeman on duty that night told a reporter: "I'll be honest with you. I was terrified. I owe my life to that nigger preacher, and so do all the other white people who were there."[48]

William White saved Douglass's life, and in doing so was himself injured. Three years after the incident in Indiana, Douglass wrote White: "I shall never forget how like two very brothers we were ready to dare, do, and even die for each other." He praised White for leaving his life of luxury, and against his father's wishes, to do "something toward breaking the fetters of the slave and elevating the despised black man." He concluded, "Dear William, from that hour...have you been loved by Frederick Douglass."[49]

****

Gandhi sent letters and personal presents to Police Superintendent Alexander and to Mrs. Alexander after they had saved his life twice in one day. Those letters are unfortunately not available.[50] Gandhi did draft letters on March 24, 1897, to the Alexanders signed by members of the Indian community. Mr. Alexander was sent a gold watch inscribed "in grateful recognition of the excellent manner in which you and your police" were able to preserve order and "were instrumental in saving the life of one whom we delight to love." The letter recognized that Mr. Alexander, in his own opinion, was doing nothing more than his duty, but the Indian community desired to express their appreciation for his efforts in "that exceptional time." £50 was also attached to be distributed to members of the police force who assisted in protecting Gandhi.

Also on March 24, 1897, a letter went out to Mrs. Alexander, who was presented with a gold watch, chain, and inscribed locket. She was praised for defending "one whom we delight to love...At no small personal risk to yourself." The letter concluded that no offering would be "an adequate return for your act which will ever be a pattern of true womanhood."[51]

Gandhi had been saved from death by a British couple who believed in justice and fair play, something often disregarded by officials in London and in South African colonies. The efforts of the Alexanders delayed his acknowledgment of the massive racial intolerance in the Colonies.

NOTES

1. Gandhi, *Autobiography*, p. 206
2. Ibid., p. 207.
3. Chapter 5 note 3 Ibid., pp. 207–08.
4. Ibid., p. 208
5. Gandhi, *Collected Works*, II:3–4. The Green Pamphlet is printed in this volume, pp. 1–52.
6. Ibid., II:9.
7. Ibid., II:14–15.
8. Ibid., II:15.
9. Ibid., II:26
10. George Hendrick and Willene Hendrick, *Black Refugees in Canada*, p. 110; Gandhi, *Collected Works*, II:26.
11. Gandhi, *Collected Works*, II:31.
12. Ibid., II:32.
13. See James Loewen, *Sundown Towns: A Hidden Dimension of American Racism*, New York: New Press, 2005.
14. Gandhi, *Collected Works*, II:47.
15. Ibid., II:94.
16. Ibid., II: 73.
17. Hine, Hine, and Harrold, *The African-American Odyssey*, p. 509.
18. Rajomohan Gandhi, *Mohandas*, p. 85.
19. Gandhi, *Autobiography*, pp. 220–21; *Collected Works*, II:377–78.
20. Gandhi, *Collected Works*, II: 220–21; Rajmohan Gandhi, *Mohandas*, 195, 201–202; Martin Green, *Gandhi*, pp. 90–93.
21. Gandhi, *Autobiography*, pp. 210–11.
22. Ibid., p. 215.
23. Gandhi, *Collected Works*, II:187–88.
24. Gandhi, *Autobiography*, p. 209.
25. Ibid., p. 209.
26. Gandhi, *Collected Works*, II:189.
27. Ibid., II:189–90.
28. Ibid., II:188–89.
29. Ibid., II:372, 382.
30. Gandhi, *Autobiography*, pp. 229–30.
31. Ibid., pp. 229–31.

32. Ibid., p. 234.
33. Ibid., p. 235.
34. Gandhi, *Collected Works*, II:194.
35. Gandhi, *Autobiography*, p. 213.
36. Gandhi, *Collected Works*, II:209.
37. Ibid., II:202.
38. Ibid., II:205.
39. Ibid., II:207–08.
40. Gandhi, *Autobiography*, pp. 236–37; *Satyagraha in South Africa*, pp. 91–96. Gandhi described mob action against him in these two accounts, with slightly different details. The two versions are combined here.
41. William S. McFeely, *Frederick Douglass*, pp. 108–12.
42. Gandhi, *Satyagraha in South Africa*, pp. 96–99; Gandhi, *Autobiography*, pp. 237–39. The two versions have slightly different details. We have combined them.
43. Philip Dray, *At the Hands of Persons Unknown: The Lynching of Black America*, pp. 116–19.
44. Gandhi, *Satyagraha in South Africa*. pp. 100–103.
45. Stephen B. Oates, *Let the Trumpet Sound*, p. 84.
46. King, *Stride Toward Freedom*, p. 136.
47. Ibid., p. 137; the telephone message from the woman about the bombing of the King home is from Lewis, *King: A Biography*, p. 70.
48. Oates, *Let the Trumpet Sound*, pp. 86–87.
49. McFeely, *Frederick Douglass*, p. 110.
50. Gandhi, *Collected Works*, II:284.
51. Ibid., II:284–85.

Chapter VI

The Transvaal and Racism

A few days after the lynching incident, Gandhi moved his family into Beach Grove Villa and resumed his busy professional life. The Natal newspapers declared Gandhi "innocent" of the charges brought against him by the mob and its organizers. His refusal to press charges against his assailants helped his reputation among some Europeans, but most citizens in Natal continued to be prejudiced against Indians, and two restrictive bills were introduced into the Natal Legislative Assembly. One restricted Indian traders, aimed at Muslims who paid their own passage to the colony. The second severely restricted Indian immigration.[1] Joseph Chamberlain, Secretary of State for the Colonies, chose to ignore the protests of Gandhi, and the British government allowed the bills to become law.

Although the British Empire had a facade of equality for all of its subjects, large numbers of Victoria's government supported South African racism. In a statement cunningly crafted, Chamberlain said that "we" sympathize with European inhabitants in the colonies who wished to prevent an "influx of people alien in civilization, alien in religion, alien in customs" of hundreds of millions of Asiatics. Immigration of Indians had to "be prevented at all hazards." He did not mention that colonists needed and desired indentured laborers of color. Chamberlain then noted that the tradition of the Empire "makes no distinction in favour of, or against race or colour; and to exclude, by reason of their colours, or by reason of their race, all Her Majesty's Indian subjects, or even all Asiatics, would be an act so offensive to those people that, it would be most painful, I am quite certain, to Her Majesty to have to sanction it."[2] Chamberlain, acting for the Queen, had sanctioned the two laws. He gave the prejudiced Natal government what it wanted, and he let the Queen be pained (except she probably didn't know about it).

****

In the 1920s when discrimination against African Americans was pervasive, the KKK and other groups opposed to immigration into the United States, except for the whitest of white groups.

****

Gandhi's victories against racism in South Africa in these early years were small; he at best won compromises which were face-saving for Indians fighting for their basic rights. Still, though often defeated, he went on vigorously representing Indian interests.

Gandhi was also facing a problem at home: his sons and young nephew needed to be educated. He was not willing to send them to the Christian mission schools, where the instruction was in English. As a special favor, he could have enrolled them in a European school, again conducted in English, and where they undoubtedly have been the only Indian children. They would have been in a hostile environment.[3]

****

When Frederick Douglass moved his family to Rochester, New York, in 1847, he enrolled daughter Rosetta, then nine years old, in the Seward Seminary where she would be taught by Miss Tracy. He was away from Rochester when school began, but upon his return asked her about her experiences as a new student. "I get along pretty well," she said, with tears in her eyes, "but father, Miss Tracy does not allow me to go into the room with the other scholars because I am colored."

Douglass, angered, called on Miss Tracy the next day; she reported that the trustees had raised objections to Rosetta's attendance. Miss Tracy proposed a compromise to them: Rosetta would be kept in a separate room for a term or more and during that time she would overcome the prejudice against her.

Douglass told Miss Tracy that he and his wife would remove Rosetta from school and that he was a national figure on the lecture circuit and editor of the North Star. Therefore, he had a platform to reveal her "unwomanly conduct."

Faced with that threat, Miss Tracy then decided to question her students, but she found the students unprejudiced. Her next move was to send a note to the parents of her students asking for comments about this racial matter. One parent objected. Because of one negative response, Miss Tracy expelled Rosetta.[4]

****

Gandhi decided to teach the children himself, but he was too busy to schedule regular instruction. He wanted the boys to speak and read Gujarati, but he failed to find a suitable teacher. Finally, he employed a governess at £7 a month, but he was dissatisfied with her work and that educational experiment ended. The boys grew up with a haphazard education, speaking Gujarati with their mother and father at home and English with Gandhi's clerks and European friends. They had desultory lessons with their father but no systematic program of study. Gandhi recognized the problem, and he wrote in his *Autobiography*: "My experiments were all inadequate....My inability to give them enough attention and other unavoidable causes prevented me from providing them with the literary education I desired, and all my sons have had complaints to make against me in this matter."[5] By 1908 when he wrote *Indian Home Rule or Hind Swaraj*, Gandhi was anti-intellectual: "I have learned Geography, Astronomy, Algebra, Geometry, etc. What of that?"[6] He condemned false education and believed education on the British model should not be compulsory, for the "ancient school system is enough."[7] He thought the "Ancient school system" was character building.

Although Mrs. Gandhi was virtually unlettered, she took up the cause of the boys' education. She was a shrewd woman and could sustain a logical argument. She was not afraid to oppose the ideas of her husband. She supported the idea of formal education for her sons, but her husband refused. He believed "Religious, that is ethical, education will occupy the first place" in educational philosophy.[8]

Gandhi believed that education of his children in England or South Africa would have been "artificial," and in an egotistical statement he wrote that "their artificial ways of living might have been a serious handicap to my public work."[9] He was willing to sacrifice the education of his sons to protect his own reputation as a champion of Indian rights.

Gandhi's work as an attorney was lucrative, but instead of indulging in luxuries he began to simplify his life. He washed and ironed his collars, he helped grind grain for bread making, he tried cutting his own hair, and he began to empty and clean his chamber pot. He was influenced by his friend Rajchandra and yearned to practice sexual abstinence, but his initial efforts failed and two more sons were born—Ramdas in 1898 and Devadas in 1900.

Gandhi obviously felt some guilt about his upper middle class life, and he also began humanitarian service. An early activity was caring for a leper who came to his door for food. Gandhi offered him shelter, dressed his limbs, and began to nurse him. The story as Gandhi tells it is incomplete, for Mrs. Gandhi undoubtedly protested that there was danger from prolonged and close contact with a leper. She would have worried about the possibility of leprosy spreading to members of the family. Gandhi did not discuss the health issues, but he writes that he could not keep the man indefinitely and sent him away to a Government Hospital for indentured laborers.[10]

The Transvaal and Racism

Nursing and medicine had long been interests of his, and he began to work with Dr. Booth, head of St. Aidan's Mission, who had established a charity hospital. The doctor used funds provided by Gandhi's friend, Mr. Rustomji. Gandhi offered his services as nurse and dispenser of medicines and was accepted. For one or two hours early in the morning, Gandhi listened to the complaints of the patients, then spoke with Dr. Booth about their medical problems. He later dispensed the medicines prescribed by Dr. Booth. Gandhi thought that this work in a charity hospital brought him peace, and it also meant he was in close contact with poor indentured laborers and their stories. Gandhi's humanitarian instincts were genuine and often practiced in his remaining years in South Africa.

Gandhi brought into Beach Grove Villa as a paying guest one of his clerks, a Christian whose parents were untouchables, the lowest caste, whose touch was thought to defile higher castes. Gandhi, as part of the many changes in his life was moving toward his later campaigns against untouchability, another part of his humanitarian work. As part of the simplification in the Gandhi family life, he and his wife were taking care of their own chamber-pots, and undoubtedly those of their younger children also. The Christian clerk, as a newcomer, was not yet attending to this matter.

Mrs. Gandhi, a traditionalist, objected to cleaning the pot of the Christian clerk and was displeased at the thought of her husband undertaking that chore. She chided him, "her eyes red with anger, and pearl drops streaming down her cheeks," Gandhi wrote, as she came down the outdoor stairway (mistranslated as "ladder" in the *Autobiography*) of the house, with chamber pot in hand.

Gandhi then clearly painted himself as an authoritarian: "...I was a cruelly kind husband. I regarded myself as her teacher, and so harassed her out of my blind love for her." He insisted it was not enough for her to carry the pot; she had to do it cheerfully.

He said, with voice raised: "I will not stand this nonsense in my house."

His words, he recalled, "pierced her like an arrow."

She shouted to him: "Keep your house to yourself and let me go."

Gandhi then interjects into this dramatic story his interpretation of his next action: "I forgot myself, and the spring of compassion dried up in me." He had forgotten himself many times before. He had mistreated his wife when she was a child bride, and for extended periods of time seems to have had almost no affection for her, favoring Mehtab.

Gandhi caught his wife by the hand and dragged her to the gate, opened it, and intended to push her out, just as in the past he had often pushed her out of his life.

With tears in torrents, Mrs. Gandhi cried out, "Have you no sense of shame? Must you so far forget yourself? Where am I to go? I have no parents or relatives here to harbour me. Being your wife, you think I must put up with your cuffs and kicks? For Heaven's sake behave yourself and shut the gate. Let us not be found making scenes like this!" She spoke truth to her demanding, inflexible husband. The implication is that had the Gandhis been in India, she would have sought refuge with her family or his family.

As we look back at her situation—and that of her children who were being denied a literary education—she and they would have had a better life had she for a few years left her husband and returned to India with the children. If she went to her husband's family in Rajkot, the boys could have attended Alfred High School as their father had done and then college or university for professional training. Mrs. Gandhi's personal life in the Gandhi family home might well have been awkward but undoubtedly less stressful than life with her husband. Had she gone to her parents' home, her life would have been easier, but there were less educational opportunities there for the children. At a later time she could have returned to Gandhi and the children, now educated, could decide to go on to work in their professions or join their father in his public endeavors. This fantasy of what might have happened did not occur.

The Transvaal and Racism 101

Gandhi was, he recalled in his *Autobiography*, ashamed of his actions and shut the gate. They could not leave each other, he wrote, and in their bickerings her endurance made her the victor. He believed, though the reader may not, that over the years he had changed: "I am no longer a blind, infatuated husband.... We are tried friends, the one no longer regarding the other as the object of lust."[11] He seems to be implying that his wife had been guilty of lust, but in most of his statements about sexual activities he declared that he was the one driven by lust. The concept of sexual love was unknown to Gandhi.

Life for Mrs. Gandhi continued to be difficult. During the Boer War (1899–1902), Gandhi invited two English friends—both Theosophists—to live with the family. Only one of the guests was named—Herbert Kitchin. Gandhi remarked without explanation: "These friends often cost my wife bitter tears."[12] Did Gandhi force her to clean their chamber-pots? Were they demanding? Rude? Kitchin was said to have a drinking problem. Was this the case when he lived with the Gandhi's? In *Satyagraha in South Africa* Gandhi noted without comment that Kitchin was a lifelong *brahmachari* (celibate).[13] Did this distress Mrs. Gandhi? It is not clear why or how these two English Theosophists caused Mrs. Gandhi's tears, but the reason or reasons must have been substantial.

Gandhi's law practice was interrupted by his service in the Boer War. The event leading to the war was the Jameson raid of 1895, four years before the beginning of the hostilities. Dr. Leander Starr Jameson, an associate of Cecil Rhodes and other wealthy businessmen, led the raid in an attempt to wrest the gold and diamond mines from the Boers and place them under British control. The raid failed, and Paul Kruger, President of the Transvaal, pardoned the plotters.

Gandhi in *Satyagraha in South Africa* wrote that the millionaires who wanted to take control of the underground riches of the Transvaal were intent in having their way, which would offer them even greater riches. Lord Milner, British High Commissioner in South Africa and Joseph

Chamberlain, Secretary of State for the Colonies, supported the British interests.

The war began in 1899, and Gandhi's personal sympathies were with the Boers because their patriarchal society resisted modern civilization. He also admired their bravery and determination in the face of all the odds against them, for the Boer forces numbered about 60,000, opposed to 350,000 Empire military forces. Gandhi's belief in nonviolence was not fully developed at this time. He approved of the warlike spirit of the Boers, opposed to the supposed cowardice of Hindus.[14]

The Indian community was divided about which side to support. Some argued that the British were oppressors of Indians, just as the Boers were. Some believed that the Boers would win the war and then wreak vengeance against Indians who supported the British.

Gandhi argued that Indians existed in South Africa only because they were British subjects. He insisted they were proud of their citizenship, and all their memorials addressing the wrongs against them because of racial attitudes all asserted their rights as subjects of the Crown.

But how should Indians support this war? Finally they decided to form a noncombat Ambulance Corps. Gandhi was the major organizer, but the formation of the corps was delayed because British officials presented many difficulties even though men were especially needed in the days when the war was going well for the Boers.[15]

The war was going badly for the British, and it was feared that Boer troops would take Durban. Dead and wounded were everywhere, and the Indian Ambulance Corps was accepted for service. Dr. Booth trained the Indian volunteers to nurse the sick and wounded. Eleven hundred Indians comprised the corps, made up of Hindus, Christians, and Muslims and included indentured laborers, professional men, and artisans.[16]

Originally, the Ambulance Corps was to serve behind the lines, but as the battles increased in intensity, the British officials asked the Indians

The Transvaal and Racism 103

to carry the wounded from the battlefield. The Ambulance Corps agreed; they often had to carry the wounded on stretchers twenty to twenty-five miles a day.

Gandhi reported that Indians in the corps often came into contact with Europeans in the British forces, and that they were treated with courtesy, even by those who had previously been opposed to Indian immigration into South Africa.[17]

****

Dr. Anderson Ruffin Abbott, a man of color born in Canada in 1837, was a medical school graduate and a friend of Dr. Augusta. Dr. Abbott was committed to black freedom and wrote Secretary of War Stanton requesting a medical appointment, to be served in a black regiment. In 1863 he was commissioned as an assistant surgeon.

Drs. Abbott and Augusta attended a levee in the East Room of the White House during the winter, 1863–1864. As the two men, in dress uniform, entered the reception room. President Lincoln came forward and took Dr. Augusta's hand. Robert Todd Lincoln, son of the Lincolns, had conservative social views. He was standing about six paces away, with his mother. He came to President, asking, "Are you going to allow this innovation?" "Why not?" Mr. Lincoln responded.

Robert Lincoln returned to stand with his mother.

Mr. Lincoln shook Dr. Augusta's hand, was introduced to Dr. Abbott, and shook his hand.

The doctors then entered the brilliantly lighted East Room, where all eyes were focused on them. Dr. Abbott later wrote, "I suppose it was the first time in the history of the U.S. when a colored man had appeared in one of these levees. What made us more conspicuous of course was our uniform. Colored men in the uniforms of U. S. military officers of high rank had never been seen before."[18]

The two doctors were given a signal honor in being received at the White House. The work of the Indian Ambulance Corps was likewise honored, with newspapers publishing rhymes ending with the refrain, "we are sons of Empire after all."[19]

****

The corps was disbanded after six weeks of service. Because the efforts of the Indians had received almost universal praise, Gandhi optimistically thought that Indian grievances would be addressed,[20] but that did not happen.

His work in the Boer war concluded, Gandhi decided in 1901 that his public work should be in India, not South Africa. As he had continued to simplify his life and to become more religious, he was increasingly opposed to the growing materialism in society. He was afraid that his main business might become making money. He wanted to devote his time to public and humanitarian work. As a concession to his supporters in South Africa, he agreed that after a year in India, should the Indian community need him, he could return.

Gifts of gold and silver and a diamond ring were bestowed on the Gandhis, and Gandhi pondered: "What right had I to accept all these gifts?" The gifts were for service to the community, but what about the gold necklace worth 80 guineas given to Mrs. Gandhi? As he thought about that problem, he argued that the necklace was given because of *his* public work. He spent a restless night, confronted by an intractable problem, for the Gandhis then had no costly ornaments.

As usual, Gandhi made the decision himself: the gifts should go to a trust which would serve the community. He drafted the necessary letter and then consulted with family members. Since he knew that he would have problems with his wife, he enlisted his sons in an effort to persuade her. The boys assured their father that their mother did not need ornaments and they certainly had no desire to possess them.

They failed to change Mrs. Gandhi's mind.

The Transvaal and Racism

It is possible to sympathize with the positions taken by Mohandas and Kasturba in the argument that followed. Gandhi, no longer an upper middle class attorney but now in the slow process of becoming a Mahatma, was facing a traditional Hindu wife not converted to his plans for some of the major changes in their lives.

She said: "You may not need them. Your children may not need them. Cajoled they will dance to your tune. I can understand your not permitting me to wear them. But what about my daughters-in-law? They will be sure to need them. And who knows what will happen tomorrow? I would be the last person to part with gifts so lovingly given." She cried.

Gandhi and the children were unmoved by her arguments and her tears.

He said: "The children have yet to get married. We do not want to see them married young. When they are grown up, they can take care of themselves. And surely we shall not have, for our sons, brides who are fond of ornaments. And if after all, we need to provide them with ornaments, I am there. You will ask me then."

She said: "Ask you? I know you by this time. You deprived me of my ornaments [to finance your education], you would not leave me in peace with them. Fancy you offering to get ornaments for the daughters-in-law. You are trying to make *sadhus* [holy men] of my boys from today! No, the ornaments will not be returned. And pray what right have you to my necklace?"

He said: "But is the necklace given you for your service or for my service?"

She said: "I agree. But service rendered by you is as good as rendered by me. I have toiled and moiled for you day and night. Is that not service? You forced all and sundry on me [probably referring to the leper, the English guests taken in by Gandhi, and her being forced into latrine duty] making me weep bitter tears, and I slaved for them!"

Some of her thrusts hit home, but Gandhi was adamant; he extorted her consent.

Mrs. Gandhi did not win the argument; her authoritarian husband did. One of his arguments, though, is compelling in our world where there is widespread public corruption: "I am definitely of opinion that a public worker should accept no costly gifts."[21]

The Gandhi family sailed to India in October 1901. Since he wanted to understand conditions in India, Gandhi attended the three day meeting of the Indian National Congress in Calcutta, but it was a great disappointment. The meetings were disorganized, the delegates had little interest in Indian mistreatment in South Africa, and the sanitary arrangements were deplorable.

Gandhi did present a resolution concerning grievances of Indians in South Africa, but it came up after 11 p.m. It had Gokhale's endorsement and passed, but it was seemingly not understood by the delegates.

As Gandhi wrote, "The Congress would meet three days every year and then go to sleep." In addition to the ineffectiveness of the Congress, which he deplored, he took on the conditions in the filthy latrines, acting as public health doctor or nurse. He tried to get cleaner latrines, but there was no support for his concerns. Gandhi made himself known to Congress delegates, but he was discouraged by the inertia he found in all aspects of the meeting.[22]

Gandhi then stayed in Calcutta for a month, meeting prominent people and explaining the problems facing Indians in South Africa. His wife and children were in Rajkot, but he writes nothing about them. His family continued to be of lesser concern than his public work.

Gandhi then spent a month with Gokhale. Since Gandhi was by this time well-along in pursuing humanitarian work and a public life, he was impressed to that Gokhale's actions were for the public good. Gokhale's major desire was for freedom for India, and he was deeply concerned by poverty in his country.[23]

During one of his walks in Calcutta, Gandhi came across a temple devoted to Kali, a goddess associated with death, disease, and destruction. She was the patroness of thugs, the religious cult of murderers and robbers. He saw a flock of sheep being taken to Kali Temple for sacrifice, and then at the temple he saw "rivers of blood." This awful sight burned into his memory. That night he had dinner with Bengali friends, and he spoke about this cruel form of worship. His friend defended animal sacrifice: "The sheep don't feel anything. The noise and the drum-beating there deaden all sensation of pain."

Gandhi objected and enunciated a view shared in many regards by animals' rights believers across the world: "I told him that, if the sheep had speech, they would tell a different tale," and he thought the practice should stop. Gandhi continued, "To my mind the life of a lamb is no less precious than that of a human being. I would be unwilling to take the life of a lamb for the sake of the human body. I hold that, the more helpless a creature, the more entitled it is to protection by men from the cruelty of man."[24] His strong expression on protection of animals is, of course, closely allied to his belief in vegetarianism.

While Gandhi was visiting Gokhale, he decided to travel third class from Calcutta to Rajkot. On that trip he came into contact with the poor of India. For years he had insisted on first class accommodations, and he now saw the overcrowding and filth on third class cars. He observed human and institutional problems: riders throwing trash on the floor, cursing, smoking, spitting; railroad owners and managers were making no efforts to improve conditions. His remedy was to have educated men travel third class and work to reform the bad habits of passengers and to complain to railway officials requesting changes in the number of passengers in the car and for the necessary cleaning. His proposal was ignored by educated men.

On the way to his family home, Gandhi stopped at the Kashi Vishvanath temple. There he found flies and noise and no sense of meditation. Nearby merchants had created a bazaar, selling toys and sweets. Stinking, rotten flowers graced the front of the temple. He searched for God "but failed to find Him."[25]

Gandhi was still developing an idealized religion, drawing ideas from Hinduism, Christianity, Islam, Jainism, Buddhism, and other faiths. Human and animal rights, high standards of ethics and morality, humanitarian efforts, and support of the poor of the earth were part of his core religious beliefs. Perhaps he saw God face to face.

****

Blacks in the United States during slavery and to the present are known for their deep religious beliefs. Historian John W. Blassingame in his classic study *The Slave Community* writes: "Most slaves, repelled by the brand of religion their masters taught, the racial inequalities in white churches, and the limitations on the bondsmen's autonomy, formulated new ideas and practices in the quarters. The true shepherd of the black flock was the slave preacher. Often one of the few slaves who could read, the black preacher was usually highly intelligent, resourceful, and noted for his powerful imagination and memory. Because of his traits of character and remarkable personality, he was able to unify the blacks, console the sick, weak, and fearful, uplift and inspire them. Suffering with his flock, he understood their tribulations and was accepted as a counselor and arbiter in the quarters. In his sermons the slaves often saw the invisible hand of God working for their earthly freedom and retribution against whites."[26]

Gandhi shared many of these qualities of the black preachers. He and King, though, did not believe in retribution against white oppressors.

***

Gokhale advised Gandhi to settle in Bombay, establish a law practice, and continue public work. Gandhi thought of his previous failures in Bombay law courts and preferred to begin in Rajkot, where he did have consider-

The Transvaal and Racism 109

able success. He then moved on to Bombay, where he took a house and chambers for his hoped-for practice. The house he had taken was "damp and ill-lighted," a curious failure on his part because of his fastidious nature. This may well have played a part in the illness of ten-year-old Manilal. The boy contracted typhoid fever, a highly contagious disease caused by contaminated water or milk and by food handlers who are carriers.

Gandhi called in a Parsi physician who determined that the boy's life was in danger and recommended eggs and chicken broth. Manilal was too young to make a decision, and Gandhi, a devoted vegetarian, determined that the use of eggs and chicken broth was unacceptable. Long interested in nursing, he decided to take command, with the help of the physician who came in to check the boy's pulse, chest, and lungs and to keep Gandhi informed about the boy's condition.

Doctors at the turn of the twentieth century certainly had no effective medicine against typhoid fever. Gandhi decided he would institute a water regimen, often giving Manilal three-minute hip-baths and orange juice mixed with water to drink.

Gandhi had little faith in regular doctors, but he was conflicted. Should he call in another physician? He asked himself a basic philosophic question: "What right had the parents to inflict their fads on their children?"

Gandhi finally concluded that "The thread of life was in the hands of God," and he decided to trust God and proceed with his own treatment. The boy was burning with fever; Gandhi wrapped him in a wet sheet and then covered him with blankets. The fever broke, and the boy began to improve. Gandhi let his *Autobiography* readers decide whether this recovery was due to God's grace, to the water cure, or the careful nursing and the liquid diet.[27]

Though there are ethical problems about refusing to follow the advice of a trained physician, Gandhi defended the vegetarian diet central to his core beliefs. He was often harsh and demanding with his children, but during Manilal's illness we see him at his best as a loving father who used effective nursing techniques to restore the boy's health.

Gandhi then moved his family from the damp, dark house into one that was well-ventilated, showing his concern for his wife and children. He was also having some success in his law practice. During this time, Gokhale often visited Gandhi's chambers, introducing friends, and inviting Gandhi to join in public work. Gandhi was feeling at ease in his profession, just as he had been in Natal.[28]

Gandhi had been in Bombay three or four months when he received a cablegram, probably from the Natal Indian Congress: "Chamberlain expected here. Please return immediately." Joseph Chamberlain was Secretary of State for the Colonies. Since Gandhi had promised he would return if there were a crisis, he closed his office, made arrangements with a male relative to stay with Mrs. Gandhi and the children in the Bombay house, and sailed for South Africa in November 1902.

When Gandhi reached Durban, he learned that the greatest problems facing Indians was then in the Transvaal. The Boers had imposed strict laws against Indians. At the end of the Boer War, with the Transvaal under the British flag, Indians believed the laws against them would be reduced. Indians purchased land in the colony but found that the revenue officer for registration would not register it. Under the new government in the Transvaal Indians were denied admission, but Europeans could get a permit for the asking.[29]

"Mr. Chamberlain," Gandhi wrote, had come to South Africa "to win the hearts of Englishmen and Boers." He was deaf to the plight of Indians. In Natal Chamberlain met with an Indian delegation, Gandhi undoubtedly having written the memorial setting forth repressions of Indians in that colony. Mr. Chamberlain gave the Indian delegation a "courteous hearing" and promised to confer with the Natal government about those problems.[30] It was an empty promise; he was determined to placate the English and the Boers.

The Transvaal and Racism   111

Mr. Chamberlain moved on to the Transvaal, and Gandhi who had lived in that colony was to follow and to be part of the delegation meeting the important government official. Gandhi, though, could not get an entry permit. He went to see his friend, Superintendent of Police Alexander, who was able to do the impossible. Gandhi left for Pretoria, the capital of the colony, where the Asiatic Department oppressed Indians.

At the end of the Boer War, British officers and soldiers from Ceylon and India came to try their luck in the roaring colony rich with gold and diamonds. The British authorities made great efforts to settle these men who were mostly soldiers of fortune. Many of these adventurers began to work for the Asiatic Department, and they saw the possibility of riches. Indians wishing a permit to enter the Transvaal might pay a corrupt official a bribe of £100. Without under-the-counter payments, Indians had almost no hope of entering the colony.[31]

****

During the years 1804–1849, the "black laws" of Ohio severely restricted black immigration. Blacks had to prove that they were free, register with a county clerk, and post a $500 bond. Most blacks were unable to meet these conditions, but local officials often ignored the "black laws."

Northern states often restricted or outlawed black voting. Connecticut had allowed black men to vote, but in 1818 passed a law permitting those blacks who had been voting to continue to do so but all others could not.

Rhode Island in 1822 refused to allow men of color to vote, but a popular uprising in 1842 repealed that law.

New Jersey in 1844 adopted a white-only voting statute in the state constitution.

The statistics on black voting in the North before 1861 are indicative of pervasive racism: 93 percent of people of color would not vote or were severely limited in that right.[32]

****

Once in Pretoria, Gandhi set to work drafting the memorial the committee would give to Mr. Chamberlain. The Asiatic Department was perplexed about how Gandhi had received a permit, for he had not paid a bribe. Had he come in illegally? If so, he could be arrested, fined, and expelled. Finally, the Asiatic Department learned how he had legally come by his permit with the assistance of Superintendent of Police Alexander.

The Asiatic Department then refused to allow Gandhi to attend the meeting with Chamberlain. Gandhi believed, with reason, that the department had coached the Secretary of State for the Colonies, who said, "I have already seen Mr. Gandhi in Durban. I therefore refused to see him here, in order that I may learn about the situation in the Transvaal at first hand from local residents." Gandhi had become the proverbial "outside agitator."

The Indian committee wanted to refuse to see Mr. Chamberlain, but Gandhi urged them to see him and present their case. He told fellow committee members, "If you do not represent your case before Mr. Chamberlain it will be presumed that you have no case at all."

The Indian delegation then called on Mr. Chamberlain, who was, Gandhi wrote "then so much under the influence of the men on the spot and so anxious was he to humour the Europeans" that he would not do justice to Indians.[33] Gandhi was correct and he was forced to continue legal battles to confront racism in the Transvaal.

****

Gandhi in his legal maneuvers to win rights for Indians was using a method later adopted by the National Association of Colored People (NAACP). Founded in 1909, the association fought for racial justice for African Americans, using the courts and a journal, *The Crisis*, to support African American rights.[34] Gandhi soon published his own newspaper.

****

The Transvaal and Racism

Gandhi decided his public work should take place in the Transvaal, and it was here that he was to formulate his method of nonviolent civil disobedience that he called Satyagraha.

Notes

1. , *Autobiography*, pp. 241–42.
2. Robert A. Huttenback, *Gandhi in South Africa*, pp. 67–68.
3. Gandhi, *Autobiography*, p. 245–48.
4. McFeely, *Frederick Douglass*, pp. 160–61.
5. Gandhi, *Autobiography*, p. 246.
6. Gandhi, *Indian Home Rule, or Hind Swaraj*, p. 89.
7. Ibid., p. 91.
8. Ibid., p. 94.
9. Gandhi, *Autobiography*, p. 246.
10. Ibid., p. 249.
11. Ibid., p. 338–40.
12. Ibid., p. 343.
13. Gandhi, *Satyagraha in South Africa*, p. 278.
14. Gandhi, *Autobiography*, p. 264; see also Gandhi, *Satyagraha in South Africa*, pp. 108–20.
15. Gandhi, *Satyagraha in South Africa*, pp. 112–19.
16. Gandhi, *Autobiography*, p. 265.
17. Gandhi wrote about the Boer War in his *Autobiography*, pp. 264–66, and in *Satyagraha in South Africa*, pp. 108–26.
18. Hendrick and Hendrick, *Black Refugees in Canada*, pp. 111–12.
19. Gandhi, *Autobiography*, p. 265.
20. Ibid., p. 266.
21. Ibid., p. 269–72.
22. Gandhi wrote about the Indian National Congress in his *Autobiography*, pp. 273–82. The quotation is from p. 274.
23. Gandhi, *Autobiography*, pp. 286–93 for an account of his meeting with Gokhale.
24. Ibid., pp. 289–90.
25. Ibid., pp. 269–97.
26. John W. Blassingame, *The Slave Community*, p. 130–31.
27. Gandhi, *Autobiography*, pp. 302–4, 306.
28. Ibid., pp. 306–7.
29. Gandhi, *Autobiography*, p. 307; Gandhi, *Satyagraha in South Africa*, pp. 129–31.
30. Gandhi, *Autobiography*, p. 311.

The Transvaal and Racism 115

31. Gandhi, *Autobiography*, pp 312–13; Gandhi, *Satyagraha in South Africa*, pp 131–32.
32. Hine, Hine, and Harrold, *The African-American Odyssey*, pp. 145–46.
33. Gandhi, *Autobiography*, p. 317; Gandhi, *Satyagraha in South Africa*, pp. 133–34.
34. Hine, Hine, and Harrold, *The African-American Odyssey*, pp. 368–69.

CHAPTER VII

GANDHI ACQUIRES
INDIAN OPINION

In Johannesburg Gandhi established a thriving law practice and developed a circle of compatible friends who began to assist him. An early disciple was Hermann Kallenbach, a German Jew born in East Prussia, an architect with advanced ideas on building who arrived in the city of gold and diamonds in 1896. He joined a busy architectural firm[1] and was a man who loved luxury. When they met, the two men talked of Buddha's renunciation. The acquaintance soon became a close friendship, and Gandhi wrote that "we thought alike, and he was convinced that he must carry out in his life the changes I was making in mine." Kallenbach began to simplify his life; once he had spent 1,200 a month on living expenses, not counting rent, and reduced that sum to 120 rupees.[2] He joined Gandhi in dietary experiments and contributed funds to Gandhi's public work and his humanitarian efforts. He was also a complete supporter of Gandhi's views and usually went along with them, without questions.

Gandhi was building a large law firm, but he was the only one who could type effectively. The two clerks he taught typing had limited English. He decided to employ a European typist, but he felt his chances were not good, for Europeans did not want to work for a colored man. A typewriter's agent sent out a Scottish lady, Miss Dick, for an interview, and she was immediately hired. In his relations with her, Gandhi was at his best. He regarded her as a daughter or sister, had complete confidence in her, and allowed her to manage large sums. She discussed with Gandhi the final choice for a husband, and he gave her away at her wedding to Mr. Macdonald. She left the office after her marriage, and Gandhi was again in need of an executive secretary.[3]

Mr. Kallenbach in 1902 then recommended Sonja Schlesin, Jewish, and about seventeen: "This girl has been entrusted to me by her mother. She is clever and honest, she is very mischievous and impetuous. Perhaps she is even insolent. You keep her if you can manage her." A feminist, Miss Schlesin spoke her mind to clients, clerks, and Gandhi himself. She had first-rate managerial skills, and like Miss Dick oversaw large accounts. Outspoken she was and deeply concerned about matters of ethical propriety. She would not accept the higher salary Gandhi offered, saying, "I am not here to draw a salary from you. I am here because I like to work with you and I like your ideals."[4] Later, during troubled times when Gandhi was in jail, she managed the nonviolent protest movement.

Another one of Gandhi's closest associates was Henry Polak, a young English-born Jew. After being educated in part in Switzerland, he came to South Africa as a sub-editor of the *Transvaal Critic*, which had a Jewish board of deputies.[5]

Gandhi, with his family still in India, lived in a room of his office and took lunch and dinner out. Polak met Gandhi in a vegetarian restaurant. The two found that they were both readers and admirers of Tolstoy and both were interested in diet and medical reform. Polak was a capable writer, a believer in racial and social justice, who recommended important books to Gandhi. Polak soon joined Gandhi as a co-worker.[6]

The three Jewish members of Gandhi's team—Schlesin, Polak, and Kallenbach—were, as Martin Green wrote in *Gandhi*, "liberal in their

Gandhi Acquires *Indian Opinion*

Judaism, and saw the history of Jews as constituting a call to them to recognize and alleviate the sufferings of similar groups." Kallenbach was also a Zionist.[7]

Gandhi's law practice was profitable, serving as it did Indian merchants, primarily Muslim, but he also represented poor Indians suffering under the restriction of the Transvaal's Asiatic Department, with its corruption, its relentless attempts to force Indians out of the Transvaal. He approved of the Indian government's refusal to permit emigration unless there was amelioration of the conditions of those Indians already in the Transvaal. He was concerned about those in "sub-human serfdom." As he matured, he slowly came to understand black Africans and to sympathize with their plight as colored people in a racist society.[8]

Another of Gandhi's Jewish friends was Louis Ritch, a Theosophist, who arranged for Gandhi to lecture at Society meetings. Ritch was manager of a business and Gandhi, needing additional help in his law practice, suggested that Ritch become articled under him.

Gandhi was especially in need for assistance after June of 1903. Sjt. Madanjit approached Gandhi about establishing a newspaper to be called *Indian Opinion*. Gandhi welcomed such a publication, and it first appeared on June 4, 1903. Originally in four languages—English, Gujarati, Tamil, and Hindi—Gandhi began to publish in the paper; he had been an avid reader of newspapers during his student years in London. He wrote quickly and precisely in English and Gujarati. The Gujarati language ones were more edgy than those on the same subject in English. His European readers could not read that language, and Gandhi could be more outspoken. Gandhi, and other contributors, vigorously presented the indignities Indians were subject to, with a plea for justice. He also began to take on a large economic burden at the paper with a small circulation, often sending £75 a month.

****

Movements need to communicate with followers and to influence general readers to the point-of-view of the sponsoring organization. In 1910 the National Association for the Advancement of Colored People (NAACP) launched its magazine *The Crisis*, edited by Dr. W.E.B. DuBois. The magazine denounced white racism and urged people of color to stand up for their constitutional rights. The Crisis was a success, with a circulation of 100,000 a month in 1918.[9]

Dr. DuBois, the Harvard-educated editor of *The Crisis* said, "I am resolved to be quiet and law abiding, but to refuse to cringe in body or soul, to resist deliberate insult, and to assert my just rights in the face of wanton aggression."[10] Likewise Gandhi was asserting the rights of Indians long before the Satyagraha movement began in 1906.

****

Both *Indian Opinion* and *The Crisis* were effective in presenting the problems faced by people of color; *The Crisis* though had more financial support from wealthy white businessmen and philanthropists and a large circulation. *Indian Opinion* had a small print run and no major financial support except for Gandhi himself.

Poor Indians who had served their indentures lived in a Johannesburg ghetto called Brickfields, where pneumonic plague broke out in 1904. Sjt. Madanjit, owner of *Indian Opinion*, was in Brickfields seeking subscribers when he discovered twenty-three Indians suffering from that highly infectious disease. The bubonic plague is spread by fleas on rats, and the pneumonic form may spread to other humans by droplets. The death rate for the disease in 1904 was extremely high. Sjt. Madanjit wrote Gandhi: "You must come immediately and take prompt measures, otherwise we must be prepared for dire consequences." He then broke into an empty house and moved the twenty-three patients there.

Gandhi cycled to the ghetto and immediately wrote the Town Clerk about the actions of Madanjit in taking possession of the house. An Indian physician, Dr. Godfrey, came to take care of the patients. More nurses were

Gandhi Acquires *Indian Opinion* 121

needed, and four of Gandhi's unmarried clerks volunteered. Mr. Ritch also wanted to join them, but he had a large family, and Gandhi did not want him to take the risk.

The Municipality praised Gandhi's intervention and sent a nurse, who came with supplies, including brandy to be taken as a precaution, as she did. Gandhi and his Indian associates had no faith in brandy and refused it.

Gandhi began an earth treatment—wet soil on the head and chest—of three patients. Two lived. The rest died, as well as the nurse. All four of Gandhi's clerks lived. Once again, we see Gandhi at his best, a humanitarian deeply concerned for poor people of color afflicted with a deadly disease. He wrote a letter to the press holding the Municipality guilty of negligence in allowing the unsanitary conditions in Brickfields to continue; therefore they were responsible for the outbreak of the plague. This letter caught the attention of Henry Polak and was responsible for his decision to meet the Indian lawyer/nurse.[11]

In 1903 Gandhi saw that he would be in South Africa for an extended period of time and decided to have his family join him. There were problems concerning a male escort, and some other delays, and the family did not arrive until late in 1904. Harilal, then sixteen, the eldest son, remained in Bombay, where he was in school. He was thinking of marriage; Gandhi gave reluctant approval to his betrothal, but was unhappy that his son had not returned to South Africa, escorting his mother and brothers.

Once again, Gandhi took a large house in an upscale neighborhood, where the family lived a simplified life for two years, grinding their own flour, cleaning their own toilet.[12] The three younger sons were not receiving a systematic education, a continuing concern of Mrs. Gandhi's. There was continuing friction within the family, for Gandhi remained opposed to formal education.

Sjt. Madanjit, publisher of *Indian Opinion*, decided to give it up, and Gandhi assumed control of the paper which had debts of about £3,500.[13] He realized he was faced with enormous financial problems, as well as the pressing need for a new editor. Fortunately, he saw possibilities in Albert West, an Englishman from a Lincolnshire farm family. He was partner in a printing shop. The two men often met at a vegetarian restaurant, but Gandhi was missing for several days while working with Indians afflicted with the plague. West sought out Gandhi early one morning to offer to help with nursing duties. Gandhi replied that the outbreak was then contained and another nurse was not needed.

"There is one thing, however," Gandhi then said.

"Yes, what is it?"

"Could you take charge of *Indian Opinion* in Durban? Mr. Madanjit is likely to be engaged here, and someone is needed in Durban. If you could go, I should feel quite relieved on that score."

"You know I have a press. Most probably I shall be able to go, but may I give you my final reply in the evening? We shall talk it over during our evening walk."

That evening, West agreed, accepting a salary of £10 a month and part of the profits, which never appeared. West and Gandhi were partners until Gandhi made his final departure from South Africa in 1914. Gandhi called West "a pure, sober, God-fearing, humane Englishman."[14] Once in Durban West discovered the dire finances of *Indian Opinion*.

Gandhi then left on a trip to Durban to study the problems of the paper. At the station, Polak gave him a copy of Ruskin's *Unto This Last* to read on the journey. Gandhi had never read a book by Ruskin before. In high school and while studying in London, he read textbooks, newspapers, and religious texts. Once he began his law practice he had little time for books, those by Tolstoy and religious works being the exceptions. Once he began reading Ruskin's book, he could not put it down. After he arrived in Durban, he spent a sleepless night: "I determined to change my life in accordance with the ideals of the book."[15]

Gandhi interpreted the message of *Unto This Last* to be:

Gandhi Acquires *Indian Opinion*

"1. That the good of the individual is contained in the good of all.

"2. That lawyer's work has the same value as the barber's, inasmuch as all have the same right of earning their livelihood from their work.

"3. That the life of labour, i.e., the life of the tiller of the soil and the handicraftsman, is the life worth living."

He arose at dawn the next day ready to put these principles into practice. He had known the first principle, the second he was dimly aware of, and the third was new to him. He believed that the second and third were contained in the first.[16]

Gandhi was convinced by Ruskin's statement that since "what one person has, another cannot have," and concluded that the rich should abstain from the luxuries of life until the poor shall have enough. Ruskin urged "not greater wealth, but simpler pleasure," a concept that Gandhi had put into practice as he had simplified his life.[17]

After making his decision, Gandhi discussed with Albert West a plan for *Indian Opinion*. The paper would be moved to a farm, on which all would work to grow food, and each worker would receive the same wage: £3 a month. Press work would be done in the spare time of the printers and press operators. West liked the idea, and so did the ten or so workers. Gandhi then advertised for land near a railway station in the vicinity of Durban and bought 100 acres for £1,000. The fertile farm named Phoenix was overgrown, though it still had some orange and mango trees, but unfortunately it was infested with many snakes.[18]

In 1904 this utopian farm, called Phoenix, influenced by Ruskin and Tolstoy, came into being. A shed was erected to hold the press. The workers at first lived in tents, then in small corrugated iron houses.[19]

Gandhi soon returned to Johannesburg to attend to his law practice, and he asked Polak to move to Phoenix to edit *Indian Opinion*. Polak resigned from *The Critic* and moved to the farm with spartan accommodations; he fully adopted the simple life there. His stay was short, for Mr. Ritch, articled to Gandhi, decided to complete his legal studies. Gandhi wanted Polak to join his legal firm and qualify as an attorney.

Gandhi was also anxious to see his young Tolstoyan Polak married and suggested that he stop delaying and marry his fiancée, Millie Graham, a Christian, who was, like her husband-to-be, attracted to the Ethical Society. The two were married in a civil ceremony that was delayed for a short time.

Gandhi was to be best man, and the Registrar of Marriages questioned the legality of the marriage, since he assumed Mr. Polak was also a man of color. Under Transvaal law at that time, a European and a colored person could not marry, and any official conducting such a ceremony was subject to heavy penalties. Gandhi took immediate action: He went to see the Chief Magistrate, a Theosophist who was a friend of Gandhi's, and explained that Polak and Miss Graham were both white. The Chief Magistrate then presided over the ceremony on December 30, 1905.[20]

The Polaks took up residence with the Gandhi family, Mrs. Polak and Mrs. Gandhi became friends, and Mrs. Polak became Mrs. Gandhi's ally, especially in matters of the education of the children and also their clothing needs. Mrs. Polak became the teacher for the boys,—giving them English lessons in reading, writing, composition, and grammar. She put forth the advantages of educating the children, but Gandhi believed "that book-knowledge obscured—if, indeed, it did not destroy—the capacity to perceive the inner vision." Mrs. Polak's arguments did not sway Gandhi, who retained his anti-intellectual views. He said, "You have no need to go to books to find God, you can find Him within yourself."[21] Gandhi did not, however, stop the lessons.

Mrs. Polak was also involved in the problem of clothing for the boys. At an earlier time, Gandhi had been insistent that the children give up traditional Indian dress, but later he changed his mind. When Mrs. Polak first lived with the family, Mrs. Gandhi was the one who wanted the children dressed nicely in Western clothes. At this stage of his life, Gandhi was indifferent or hostile to the idea. Mrs. Gandhi would ask Mrs. Polak to make the case to replenish worn clothing. Mrs. Polak would tell Gandhi "that the children must have the things to equip them for their time and place." Gandhi would counter argue that he "never wanted the boys to have possession or to be taught to think of things that might obscure the simple vision of the soul's need."[22] Mrs. Polak would argue with Gandhi, but she was seldom successful.

Mrs. Polak supplies a detailed picture of the dinner hour of the household. For the first time that day, all family members were together, and usually there were guests. From ten to fourteen people were present. The meal was simple: the first course was vegetable dishes, raw salad, lentils, whole meal bread, and peanut butter. The second course would be a milk dish and uncooked fruit, with cereal coffee or lemonade. The conversation was light, with jest and wit predominating. Gandhi had a highly developed sense of humor, but he also included serious talk at the dinner table. Gandhi was often autocratic when dealing with his wife and children, but he was a charming host at his home.[23]

Mrs. Gandhi was often portrayed negatively in her husband's *Autobiography*, but Mrs. Polak saw her in a different light, as a woman with strong principles. Some Europeans, whom Gandhi knew casually and Mrs. Gandhi not at all, invited themselves to dinner. Once they arrived and before dinner was served, they were "rudely curious" about the home life of the Gandhi family, asking intimate questions arrogantly. Gandhi seemed not to be offended and set forth the reality instead of rumors about Indian life. Mrs. Gandhi was angry about these callous people, and she disappeared from the drawing room. When she did not appear at the dinner table, Gandhi went upstairs in search of her, but she refused to join the group. The next day she told Mrs. Polak that she would not have people come to the house for "idle curiosity" and to "make laugh" at her and her home. If they came, she would not see them.[24] Gandhi was still, in part, an

Anglo-Indian gentleman who met indignities from Europeans with facts and a smile. Mrs. Gandhi was different.

Four months after the Polaks were married, the Polaks and the Gandhi family left Johannesburg for the austerity of the Phoenix Farm. Mrs. Polak believed the move, in part, was Gandhi's attempt to live an even simpler life. Gandhi in his *Autobiography* gives a different reason for the move. When the Zulu Rebellion broke out in 1906, he wrote the Natal government offering to form an Indian Ambulance Corps. The offer was accepted, and he decided to move to the rustic farm.

Gandhi had no grudges against Zulus, for they had not harmed Indians. Indeed, Indian hawkers did a flourishing business with them. Against all evidence to the contrary, Gandhi then believed that the British Empire "existed for the welfare of the world."[25] He recruited twenty-three men; most were Hindus, but six were Muslims. He was appointed Sergeant Major, and he had under him three sergeants and one corporal. The corps was in service for six weeks. Once he arrived at the scene, he saw that there was nothing to justify the term of "rebellion," the word used to describe the conflict. A Zulu chief had advised the non-payment of a tax being imposed by the British and killed the sergeant who came to collect that tax. The hostilities began. The British retaliated with machine guns, floggings, and hangings. The Zulus being treated by Gandhi and his men had not been wounded in battle. Some were suspects who had been captured and ordered flogged by a general. Others had been given badges indicating they were not enemies, but they were shot by British soldiers by mistake.[26]

The wounds of the Zulus were festering, and most of the Europeans serving in the armed forces would not nurse them, but the Indians did. European soldiers tried to persuade the Indians from assisting the Zulus, and when they did not, these soldiers "poured unspeakable abuse on the Zulus."[27] Had the Indian Corps not been present, many Zulus would have been left to die.

****

British troops were not restrained from brutalizing Zulus and faced no penalties for their actions. Similarly slaves in the United States were beaten or flogged, and no legal actions were taken against the masters or their representatives. John Little, a slave in North Carolina, was sold to a neighbor on a nearby plantation. His new owner was known as a slave "breaker"—that is one who forced slaves into submission, just as Zulus were being forced into submission.

Little, without permission, went back to his birthplace to see his mother one week-end, returning Sunday. Monday morning two slaves and an overseer captured him, tied him to an apple tree, and called for the master, who ordered the overseer to give Little 500 lashes. The slaves then undressed Little, pulling his shirt over his head, effectively blindfolding him. Before the whipping began, the master used his cane to show where the lashes were to go: "Whip him from there down."

The master counted the blows given by the overseer. By the count of 100, Little felt no sensation. The master then said, "Now, you cursed, infernal son of a b---, your running about will spoil all the rest of my niggers...."

Little tried to explain, but the master struck the slave on the head with his cane and told the overseer to continue. Little did not know how many blows he received from the bull whip, but "from the small of my back to the calves of my legs, they took the skin clear off, as you would skin beef." A slave then washed him with salt water, causing great misery.[28]

Little's master had nothing to fear for ordering this brutal beating. Law officials looked the other way. White soldiers in the British army who were mistreating Zulus had nothing to fear from their officers, for Zulus were considered less than human. Though Zulus received dastardly treatment and British soldiers had no qualms about allowing their festering wounds to kill them, slaves were valuable, and masters, even the cruelest ones, would stop harsh treatment short of death. There are, though, some few cases in which slaves were beaten to death by their masters.

****

Gandhi and his men were also involved in the care of European soldiers, He had worked as nurse/pharmacist in Dr. Booth's hospital, and as needed he prepared prescriptions for the white soldiers. He served both whites and blacks with equal care.

Though Gandhi did not describe the cruelties to Zulus, he did write: "This was no war but a man-hunt.... To hear every morning reports of the soldiers' rifles exploding like crackers in innocent hamlets, and to live in the midst of them, was a trial."[29] It was during this horrible war against the Zulus that Gandhi began to think again about abstinence from sexual activities. He had been attempting to abandon sexual relations with his wife for some six years. He reported that he had failed twice, perhaps a reference to the conception of his last two children.

During the long marches, his mind dwelt on Raychand's praise of celibacy. He came to the conclusion that in years to come he would have even more occasions for humanitarian service, and he could not fulfill these public service duties if he continued to propagate and rear children.[30] Highly sexed and refusing to use contraceptive methods, Gandhi had tried sleeping in a different bed from his wife's and had experimented with various food reforms. Finally, in 1906, he took a vow during the Zulu Rebellion to be chaste. With all the zeal of a reformer, once he reached Phoenix after being demobbed, he spoke with some of the settlers and West about foregoing sexual activity. Some agreed and became celibate. Gandhi was vague in his comments, suggesting that many of his associates did not wish to forego sex. He spoke with his wife about his vow, but her reaction is not known.

What Gandhi did report in his *Autobiography* was that "The difficulties are even today staring me in the face."[31] His later life would not have been haunted by sexual denial had he believed that sex could be a part of love, that sex was not necessarily lust.

Gandhi Acquires *Indian Opinion*

In his role as powerful husband, Gandhi took the vow of chastity without discussing this momentous decision with his wife. She had few alternatives. Divorce was not possible.

As described by Mrs. Polak, life at Phoenix was often bleak. The railway station was 14 miles from Durban, and then there was a trek of two miles from the Phoenix station to the farm. The buildings were primitive, built of corrugated iron, without insulation, and were suffocatingly hot at times. The dwellings were small: living room/dining room together, bedroom or bedrooms, kitchen, lean-to bath. Roofs were flat, and colonists often slept there.

On the top of the bathroom roof was a watering can. There was a hole in the roof; pull a cord, the can turned, water flowed down. Each house had an outdoor toilet, with bucket. Occupants were responsible for emptying the bucket at the approved place.

Mrs. Polak pointed out in *Mr. Gandhi the Man* that utopian settlements seemed reasonable and doable on paper, but in practice there were problems large and small. Neighboring mules and donkeys were not stabled at night and ate the vegetables in the gardens of the colonists. Water was at a premium, captured as it was from roof tops in large water-butts. Snakes, some of which were poisonous, were much in evidence, and Gandhi was opposed to killing them. There were many arguments. Gandhi believed that husbands had absolute control over wife and children. Mrs. Polak strenuously disagreed.[32]

Mrs. Polak gives valuable details about the settlers at Phoenix. The original ones were involved in the editing and production of *Indian Opinion* and were all paid the same salary.

The planned school was to teach some elementary subjects but would concentrate on character building and on the child's own inner self. No dogmas were to be taught. The school was slow to be formed, and once again the Gandhi children and the children of settlers were often receiving a haphazard or no education.

Reflecting one of Gandhi's interests, there was to be a house of healing using natural means—rest, fasting, enemas, steam baths, mudpacks.

West did organize a smooth printing organization. Gandhi provided copy in English and Gujarati; Mr. Polak and others who came into Gandhi's orbit also contributed their writing and editing skills, but the utopian settlement certainly had problems:[33] money was scarce, there were personal disagreements and feuds, and Gandhi's willingness to undertake fads kept some pioneers on edge. What foods were to be avoided? Milk? Legumes? How simple should the simple life be? The problems persisted, but the experiment continued.

The expenses for the entire *Indian Opinion* operation were extensive, and Gandhi made up the deficits. That meant he had to spend much of his time in Johannesburg making money at his law office in order to support Phoenix and *Indian Opinion*. His wife and children were free from coping with his problems, including the neglect of the education of his sons. He began to live with Kallenbach, probably platonically.

****

Rev. Dr. Martin Luther King, Jr., came to national prominence after Rosa Parks refused to give up her seat on a Montgomery, Alabama, bus, putting into motion the civil rights movement. To raise the necessary funds for the movement, King spent much of his time travelling and giving speeches and raising money. His personal life suffered greatly and his marriage was reported strained, no doubt caused in part by the rumors that he had female companions when he was on those speaking trips. Gandhi's efforts for his fellow Indians damaged his family life, causing his wife and children to suffer.

****

While Gandhi was still in the Indian Ambulance Corps, he received a copy of the proposed anti-Indian ordinance known as "the Black Act." He saw immediately that if the ordinance passed and Indians acquiesced, it "would spell absolute ruin for the Indians in South Africa."[34] He felt

Gandhi Acquires *Indian Opinion* 131

Indians should protest, for it would be better to die than to submit to such a law. He recognized that he faced an impenetrable wall of racism and segregation. At this same time in the United States in 1906, blacks faced the same impenetrable wall.

The proposed ordinance was shocking in its attacks on members of the British Empire. The Registrar on the new registration card of an Indian would note identifiable marks and take finger and thumb prints. Minor children and women would also be covered by the same procedures. Once the new certificate of registration was issued, any police officer could, at any time and in any circumstance, demand to see it. If the certificate were not produced, the Indian could be fined, deported or sent to prison. Police could enter private homes to check for certificates.[35] Indians were being treated as criminals, and the proposed Ordinance would force many Indians to leave the country, something desired by Transvaal leaders.

A mass meeting to discuss the Ordinance was called for the Empire Theatre in Johannesburg on September 11, 1906. The Fourth Resolution was the most important one. In it, Indians solemnly agreed not to obey it should it become law and to suffer the penalties of non-compliance.[36] Sheth Haji Habid spoke with passion about the resolution and declared that "we must pass this resolution with God as witness and must never yield a cowardly submission to such degrading legislation." He went on to declare that "in the name of God" he would not submit and asked those in attendance to do the same.[37]

Gandhi had been unaware of the content of Habid's speech but immediately seized the moment, seeing that taking such an oath would assist Indians showing a united front against this racial legislation.

The resolution passed.

****

After Rosa Parks was arrested on December 1, 1955, for refusing to give up her seat to a white man, black people the following Monday staged a boycott of the bus system in Montgomery, Alabama. The event was an enormous success, with black riders sharing rides, walking, or taking a cab. That afternoon black leaders met to discuss a mass meeting to be held that night at the Holt Street Baptist Church. Some at the meeting requested secrecy, afraid of reprisals. To that, E. D. Nixon, the fiery NAACP member, responded: "Let me tell you gentlemen one thing. You ministers have lived off these wash-women for the last hundred years and ain't never done anything for them." Nixon exposed the weaknesses of ministers in a segregated society. They had gone along with the system, no matter their personal dislike of racism. They were like the Indian businessmen Gandhi first met in South Africa who accepted the racism in South Africa because they were making profits.

Nixon continued to taunt those blacks who did not protest segregation: "We've worn aprons all our lives. It's time to take the aprons off. If we're gonna be mens [sic], now's the time to be mens. [sic]"[38]

Dr. King arrived late, as Nixon was concluding. He seized the attention of those planning the night meeting: "Brother Nixon, I'm not a coward. I don't want anyone to call me a coward."[39] He then argued that the leaders should act in an open fashion and use their own names in their resolutions.

Dr. King seized an opportunity, and he was elected president of the Montgomery Improvement Association. That night, in a rousing speech, Dr. King asked black people to continue the protest.[40] He did not ask members of the audience to take a religious vow as Indians in Johannesburg did on September 11, 1906, but most of those in the Holt Street church were religious, and the meeting was in a house of worship, adding a religious dimension to the protest movement.

****

Gandhi was aware that he needed to have support of all the different Indian religious groups there, and he declared, "We all believe in one and the same God, the differences in nomenclature in Hinduism and Islam notwithstanding."[41] (It is certainly debatable that the audience members all believed in the same God, and there were continuing tensions between Hindus and Muslims as the protest movement developed.) Gandhi declared that he would rather die than submit to the racist Ordinance.[42]

Then, at the end of the meeting, all of those present "with upraised hands, took an oath with God as witness not to submit to the Ordinance if it became law."[43]

The movement, first to be called "Passive Resistance," was beginning.

Notes

1. Martin Green, *Gandhi*, p. 210; Joseph Lelyveld, *Great Soul*, pp. 88–97.
2. Gandhi, *Autobiography*, pp. 401–02.
3. Ibid., pp. 344–45.
4. Ibid., pp. 345–46; *Satyagraha in South Africa*, pp. 275–76.
5. Martin Green, *Gandhi*, p. 208–09.
6. Gandhi, *Autobiography*, p. 363.
7. Martin Green, *Gandhi*, p. 207; Lelyveld, *Great Soul*, p. 94.
8. Gandhi, Collected *Works*, 4:vii.
9. John Hope Franklin and Alfred A. Moss, Jr., *From Slavery to Freedom*, p. 353.
10. Hine, Hine, and Harrold, *The African-American Odyssey*, pp. 368–69.
11. Gandhi, *Autobiography*, pp. 354–55.
12. Rajmohan Gandhi, *Mohandas*, pp. 112–14.
13. Martin Green, *Gandhi*, p. 216.
14. Gandhi, *Autobiography*, pp. 358–59.
15. Ibid., pp. 364–65.
16. Ibid., pp. 364–65; see also Rajmohan Gandhi, *Mohandas*, pp. 134–35. Gandhi's paraphrase of Ruskin's *Unto This Last* was published by Navajivan Publishing House in 1951.
17. One of the best discussions of Gandhi and Ruskin is found in Louis Fischer, *The Life of Mahatma Gandhi*, pp. 67–68.
18. Gandhi, *Autobiography*, pp. 366–68; Millie Graham Polak, *Mr. Gandhi the Man*, pp. 36–46.
19. Gandhi, *Autobiography*, pp. 366–68.
20. Ibid., p. 377; see also Polak, *Mr. Gandhi the Man*, pp. 13–14.
21. Polak, *Mr. Gandhi the Man*, pp. 14, 22–23.
22. Ibid., p. 22.
23. Ibid., p. 23.
24. Ibid., p. 24.
25. Gandhi, *Autobiography*, p. 383.
26. Ibid., pp. 384–85; Martin Green, *Gandhi*, p. 218; Rajmohan Gandhi, *Mohandas*, p. 116–17.
27. Gandhi, *Autobiography*, p. 304.
28. Hendrick and Hendrick, *Black Refugees in Canada*, pp. 120–21.
29. Gandhi, *Autobiography*, pp. 385–86.

30. Ibid., p. 386.
31. Ibid., p. 387.
32. Polak, *Mr. Gandhi the Man*, pp. 42–51.
33. Ibid., p. 37.
34. Gandhi, *Satyagraha in South Africa*, p. 155.
35. Ibid., p. 156–59.
36. Ibid., p. 161.
37. Ibid., p. 162.
38. Taylor Branch, *Parting the Waters*, p. 136.
39. Ibid., pp. 136–37.
40. Ibid., pp. 138–41.
41. Gandhi, *Satyagraha in South Africa*, p. 165.
42. Ibid., p. 168
43. Ibid., p. 169.

Chapter VIII

Love

An Interlude

His marriage unhappy, his relationship with his children uneasy, Gandhi and the German-born architect Hermann Kallenbach became soul mates, and Gandhi moved in with him. Gandhi had ceased having sexual relations with his wife in 1906, and about that time for the next few years he became Kallenbach's housemate. Off and on, they seem to have been together for about three years.

Kallenbach was deeply influenced by Gandhi's views on chastity, on the need for a simple life, and for a life of poverty. He wrote his brother in 1908, "For the last two years I have given up meat eating...for the last 18 months I have given up my sex life....I have changed my daily life in order to simplify it."[1] The nature of his previous sex life is not known.

The story of these two soul mates, both living in the strange world of South Africa, was first told, in any detail, in Joseph Lelyveld's *Great Soul: Mahatma Gandhi and His Struggle with India*. Gandhi destroyed Kallenbach's letters, but Kallenbach saved Gandhi's letters, now published in volume 96 of *The Collected Works of Mahatma Gandhi*. The letters show the relationship of these two men to be, as Lelyveld in *Great Soul* has said, "intimate" and "ambiguous."[2]

In his *Autobiography*, *Satyagraha in South Africa*, and other writings devoted to his life in South Africa, Gandhi speaks admiringly of Kallenbach's personal qualities and his support of the Indian cause but gives no indication of the complicated personal relationship they had. This is strange for in his *Autobiography* he wrote at length about his erotic, difficult relationship with Mehtab, without using Mehtab's name, and perhaps not fully understanding the nature of that tangled web of deceit discussed in earlier chapters.

Gandhi's letters to Kallenbach are, in part, playful. He is the Upper House and Kallenbach the Lower House. The dominant Upper House dictates to the lesser one, gives advice, and expects to be obeyed. Kallenbach usually followed Gandhi's wishes; he eagerly gave up his extravagant ways for a life of poverty, stopped eating meat, gave up his sex life, but he did not part with his expensive automobile and did not, as Gandhi kept requesting, leave his architecture practice.

Gandhi's playfulness is capable of more than one interpretation. In a letter of July 29, 1911, Gandhi wrote Kallenbach who was soon leaving for Europe to see relatives, and he was told not to marry. Gandhi expected him to spend prudently, and he continued: "Lower House shall not look lustfully upon any woman." Was this a comic reference, given Kallenbach's statement that he had given up sex, or was Gandhi insisting that Kallenbach remain faithful to him?

In that same letter, Gandhi set forth other tasks and then ends, "The consideration for all the above tasks imposed by Lower House on himself is more love and yet more love between the two Houses—such love as, they hope, the world has not seen. In witness whereof the parties hereto solemnly affix their signatures in the presence of the Maker of all this 29th day of July at Tolstoy Farm."[3] What is the reader to make of a solemn promise, before God, for love and more love?

Earlier, on September 10, 1909, Gandhi had written: "I have another charming letter from you. Everyone considers that your love for me is excessive. I pass on the thought for what it may be worth."[4] "Everyone" was probably the circle of supporters around Gandhi, jealous of Kallenbach.

The circle around Gandhi was apparently a hotbed of jealousies. On September 24, 1909, from London, Gandhi assured Kallenbach of his love: "Your portrait (the only one) stands on my mantelpiece in the bedroom. The mantelpiece is opposite to the bed." He continued, "cotton-wool and vaseline are a constant reminder"[5] of Kallenbach. Lelyveld speculates that the Vaseline possibly refers to its usage in giving enemas, part of Gandhi's health regime, and in massage, favored by Gandhi.[6] That sentence implies, if Lelyveld's speculation is correct, that Kallenbach played a part in enema giving and massage, both of which can be erotic. Vaseline, however, is also used in anal sex. Gandhi and Kallenbach had become chaste, but love is powerful. Before 1906 Gandhi had twice failed to refrain from sexual activities with his wife. Was this mutual attraction of soul mates strong enough for them to break their chastity vows? The letters do not provide conclusive evidence; given Gandhi's squeamishness about sexual matters, the two were probably platonic lovers.

When Gandhi was disturbed because a close associate had taken a large sum of money without permission, he wrote Kallenbach on February 14, 1914: "I do feel like taking you away and both of us escaping to the jungle. What a snare and delusion this wretched civilization, in the midst of which you and I are now living and of the bitter fruit of which we are still tasting! Woe to us if we tarry in it for a minute longer than may be absolutely necessary."[7]

Gandhi, Mrs. Gandhi, and Kallenbach were leaving for India in 1914, with a stop first in London. World War I began, interfering with plans. Kallenbach, as a German national, was not allowed to leave England. Mr. and Mrs. Gandhi did continue, and Gandhi and Kallenbach did not meet again in 1937, in India. Kallenbach in 1937 referred to his life with Gandhi as living "almost in the same bed,"[8] but he did not elaborate.

The large number of letters covering the years 1908–1914 take up almost 200 pages in volume 96 of *The Collected Works of Mahatma Gandhi*. They are sometimes painful as Gandhi writes about his personal problems with wife, children, and South African government officials. He was far more uncertain, more conflicted, that he was in his formal writing. The letters do indicate the two men were soul mates but leave open the question: Were they physical or platonic lovers? While that question is unanswered, it is obvious that Gandhi loved Kallenbach more than he did Mrs. Gandhi, who had been chosen by parents to be his child bride. He and Kallenbach chose each other and appear to have lived together harmoniously. Given Gandhi's squeamishness about sexual matters, that relationship was probably platonic.

NOTES

1. Quoted in Joseph Lelyveld, *Great Soul*, p. 90.
2. Ibid., p. 88.
3. Gandhi, *Collected Works*, 96:62–63.
4. Ibid., 96:26.
5. Ibid., 96:28.
6. Lelyveld, *Great Soul*, p. 89.
7. Gandhi, *Collected Works*, 96:161.
8. Lelyveld, *Great Soul*, p. 88.

Chapter IX

Smuts's Betrayal and the Consequences

An optimist, Gandhi believed that if the Imperial Government understood the plight of Indians in the Transvaal, then a Crown colony, the Black Act would be rejected by the Crown. Acting upon this delusion, Indians selected a two-man delegation—Gandhi and Haji Ojer Ali, a well-known Muslim merchant—to go to London to present the Indian case. The two men sailed for England in early October, 1906. Once in London, Gandhi set about trying to influence public opinion and high government officials. Mr. Ali was ill most of the six week stay, but Gandhi did the work of a dozen men, meeting officials, preparing memorials, and writing letters—about 5,000 in all—and giving interviews.[1]

Gandhi did convince a few people of the injustices suffered by Indians in the Transvaal, but there were few cracks in the Empire in 1906. Most British citizens and officials had no qualms about the conditions of people of color in the colonies. The wealth from imperialism was more important.

Lord Elgin, Secretary of State for the Colonies, splendidly played his role in a charade. He listened to the presentation of the deputation "with attention" and "expressed his sympathy," promising to do all he could.[2] Lord Elgin, though, told Sir Richard Solomon, the Transvaal representative then in London, that he would not recommend assent of the Ordinance, but the Transvaal would be granted self-government on January 1, 1907, and could act as it wished. Sir Richard was pleased by the decision, for he knew, and Lord Elgin knew, what the Transvaal government would do. In the spirit of this decision, the betrayal was kept secret from Mr. Gandhi, Mr. Ali, and the British public.

During his stay in London, Gandhi met with suffragettes working against massive opposition for women's rights. They were using passive resistance at a time when Gandhi was thinking about possible forms of action once the Black Act went into effect. The resistance of these women made a powerful impression on Gandhi.[3]

When Gandhi and Mr. Ali left England, they could be both optimistic and pessimistic. Lord Elgin had given the delegation a fair hearing, or so they thought, but they were also aware of pressure in the Transvaal to enact the Black Act. When the ship they were on reached Madeira, they received a telegram from Mr. Ritch, formerly articled to Mr. Gandhi in Johannesburg and then studying in London, indicating that Lord Elgin was unable "to advise his Majesty the King that the Transvaal Asiatic Ordinance should be brought into operation."[4]

For the rest of the trip to South Africa, Gandhi and friends were living in a false paradise, w1th no suspicions of the crooked policy. Once the ship arrived in South Africa, Gandhi and Ali discovered the agreement made by Lord Elgin and Sir Richard. The Black Act was going to become law, and it did. What Gandhi finally learned was that Indians in the Transvaal could expect no help from the Imperial Government to protest the racist laws and activities in the colonies.[5] Gandhi came to this realization before the protest movement went beyond a religious oath to disobey the Black Act.

Smuts's Betrayal and the Consequences 145

After January 1, 1907, the Transvaal government passed the Black Act, which would go into effect on July 1, 1907. Indians did not sit idly by for six months; they organized a "Passive Resistance Association," later renamed the "Satyagraha Association." Gandhi came to the realization that passive resistance implied weakness.

After Gandhi began to spend large portions of his income on the movement, he stopped sending money to his older brother Laxmidas for support of the extended family in Rajkot. After his brother asked for funds, Gandhi wrote in a belligerent way that he could not do so, asserting that his family now consisted of all living things. He had repaid the 13,000 rupees used for his study in London and much else.

The two Gandhi brothers were estranged for many years. Part of the tension between them was Gandhi's fault, for he did not carefully explain the meaning and importance of the Satyagraha movement. Gandhi expected his brother to accept his decrees and follow them meekly.

The powerful Transvaal government was faced by 13,000 Indians, most of whom were opposed to the racist legislation. Some Indian merchants, however, were willing to register in order to keep their profitable businesses. Registration was to end on November 30, 1907. To Gandhi's dismay, some members of the Indian community made threats against those planning to register, or those who had already done so. Gandhi tried to stop threats and reprisals. Eventually, just over 500 Indians, largely Muslims, registered, many at night to hide their cowardice.[6]

There were strains in the community between Hindus and Muslims then. On June 22, 1907, *Indian Opinion* began a series to preserve unity between the two religious groups. To "spread education and culture" among the entire Indian community, the paper would publish sections of Washington Irving's *Life of the Prophet*. Gandhi wrote that most Hindus were ignorant of the life and career of the Prophet, and most Muslims were unaware of researches on the Prophet by English speaking writers.[7]

Gandhi believed in freedom of the press, speech, and religion, all controversial in his society.

Indian Opinion on August 31, 1907, announced that the series of translated portions of the *Life of the Prophet* had been cancelled. The opening sections of Irving's book were about "idol-worship, superstition and evil customs prevalent in Arabia before the Prophet was born." Muslim readers of *Indian Opinion* did not want to read "any such life of the Prophet." Gandhi defended the translation of Irving's biography, but in order to placate Muslims decided to stop publishing it.[8] The episode might appear trivial, but it suggests the difficult relationships between Hindus and Muslims in South Africa and later in India.

During the period of unease between July 1 and November 30, when registration was to end, Gandhi read a copy of Henry Thoreau's essay "Resistance to Civil Government," (1849) commonly called "Civil Disobedience." The edition he read was published as a pamphlet by Arthur C. Fifield in his "Simple Life" series. More than likely Henry Polak passed the essay on to Gandhi, who was deeply impressed by it.[9]

The first mention in *Indian Opinion* of Thoreau's essay was a brief one in English on September 7, 1907, concerning passive resistance in England as a method of securing redress as "the only course law-abiding and peaceful men can adopt without doing violence to their conscience." Ostensibly, the article on civil disobedience was about the bill legalizing in England the marriage with a deceased wife's sister, which was converting the clergy of the Established Church into resisters. The Archbishop of Canterbury had issued a message requesting the clergy not to celebrate such unions, though they were now recognized as legal. Gandhi applied the news story to the situation of Indians in the Transvaal and quoted Thoreau's essay: "If one were to tell me that this was a bad Government because it taxed certain foreign commodities brought to its ports, it is most probable that I should not make any ado about, for I can do without them. All machines have friction, and possibly this does enough good to counterbalance the evil. At any rate, it is a great evil to make a stir about it. But when the friction comes to have its machine, and oppression and robbery are paramount, I say let us not have any such machine any longer."

Gandhi intuitively understood Thoreau's words, for he recognized that in the Black Act, Indians "have not only a law which has some evil in it, that is to say, using Thoreau's words, a machine with friction in it, but it is evil legalised, or it represents friction with machinery provided for it." Gandhi then referred to the oath, with God as witness, not to obey the Black Act: "Resistance to such an evil is a divine duty which no human being can with impunity disregard, and, as in the case of the Archbishop of Canterbury, so in that of British Indians, it is their conscience that must decide, as it has already decided, whether to submit to the Asiatic Act or not, cost what it may."[10]

Gandhi published "Duty of Disobeying Laws" in the Gujarati section on September 7, 1907: "Many years ago, there lived in America a great man named Henry David Thoreau. His writings are read and pondered over by millions of people." Gandhi's second sentence was certainly not true in 1907, but it was to become true by the end of the century. Some of Thoreau's readers, he continued, "put his ideas into practice. Much importance is attached to his writings because Thoreau himself was a man who practised what he preached." Gandhi was impressed that Thoreau not only opposed slavery but took steps against that institution: "He was imprisoned when he stopped paying the taxes due from him. The thoughts which occurred to him during this imprisonment were boldly original and were published in the form of a book." Gandhi was wrong when he wrote, "Historians say the chief cause of the abolition of slavery in America was Thoreau's imprisonment and the publication by him of the above-mentioned book after his release." Thoreau's essay on "Civil Disobedience" was little read and understood during his lifetime. Thoreau was influenced by the abolitionist leader William Lloyd Garrison, and the Garrisonians did play a role in the struggle to end slavery. Gandhi recognized that Thoreau's "example and writings are at present exactly applicable to the Indians in the Transvaal." Gandhi then shrewdly chose some of the best quotations from "Civil Disobedience" such as, "I accept that government is best which governs least. That is, government is a kind of disease and the greater the freedom people enjoy from it, the more admirable the government." (The quotation is far from accurate, perhaps because of the translation into Gujarati and then back into English.) Gandhi then quoted about 500 more words from Thoreau, all applicable to the situation Indians faced after November 30, 1907, if they did not register.[11]

The next week, September 14, 1907, Gandhi published more translations into Gujarati from Thoreau's "Civil Disobedience," including this paragraph: "Under a government which imprisons any unjustly, the true place for a just man is also a prison. Hence, the proper place today for good people in Massachusetts is in her prisons. In a slave State prison is the only house in which a free man can abide with honour. If they think that in that case their influence will be lost and none will be left to fight injustice, they do not know how to fight evil. They do not know how much stronger truth is than error. Those who are in gaol, suffering the tyranny of injustice, can combat injustice more effectively from there than outside. So long as a minority conforms to the majority, it is not even a minority. They must throw in their whole weight in the opposite direction."[12] (Again, Gandhi paraphrases and puts together similar ideas from different parts of the essay.)

Gandhi also published from the famous paragraph in which Thoreau states that the state could punish his flesh for his refusal to support slavery. Although he was confined, he felt free, and his views about the State "became more dangerous" and he lost all remaining respect for it.[13] Gandhi had learned from his experiences with Lord Elgin that the State would not respect and support its Indian citizens.

In the English section of *Indian Opinion* for October 26, 1907, Gandhi described Thoreau as "a great writer, philosopher, poet" who acted on his beliefs and was one of America's greatest moral men. He recognized that Thoreau went to jail "for the sake of his principles and suffering humanity." The appeal is clear here, for Gandhi saw that the essay had been "sanctified by suffering." Gandhi had not suffered yet for his beliefs, but he recognized, a month before the registrations of Indians was to be completed that his incarceration might be a possibility.[14]

Gandhi wrote Henry Salt that the essay on "Civil Disobedience" was so compelling he wanted to know more about Thoreau and he read Salt's *Life of Henry David Thoreau*,[15] probably the 1896 edition, and Thoreau's short essays, probably Salt's edition of *Anti-Slavery And Reform Papers* (1890), and *Walden*. Just when he read these Thoreau works is not known, but was likely soon after he read "Civil Disobedience." Gandhi followed his interests quickly and undoubtedly had Polak search the Johannesburg bookstores for the Thoreau texts. From Salt's biography, Gandhi would have learned that Thoreau collected and read the sacred scriptures of India, including the *Bhagavad-Gita*, Gandhi's own favorite. From *Anti-Slavery and Reform Papers*, Gandhi would have read other powerful essays about the evils of slavery.

In *Walden*, Gandhi would certainly have been impressed by Thoreau's simple life and his mysticism, especially this passage: "Sometimes, in a summer morning, having taken my accustomed bath, I sat in my sunny doorway from sunrise till noon, rapt in a revery...until by the sun falling in at my west window, or the noise of some traveller's wagon on the distant highway, I was reminded of the lapse of time....They were not time subtracted from my life, but so much over and above my usual allowance. I realized what the Orientals meant by contemplation and the forsaking of works."[16] Gandhi would have realized again why he was attracted to Thoreau, who identified himself in one brief paragraph as being a Hindu yogi.

Gandhi did not read Thoreau until late in the summer of 1907, a year after the meeting at the Empire Theatre on September 11, 1906, at which time members of the Indian community took an oath, with God as witness, not to accept the terms of the proposed Black Act. Gandhi did read Thoreau in those critical months before registration was completed on

November 30, 1907 and before he went to jail. Thoreau was s kindred spirit, and his essay on resistance influenced Gandhi just before the jailings began, and then later while he was jailed.

During this watchful waiting period before the Black Act went into full effect, Gandhi was concerned about the use of the term "passive resistance." The term was not correct, because nonviolent resistance was active. A small prize was announced in *Indian Opinion* to the person who invented the best word for the struggle. His relative Maganlal Gandhi suggested *Sadagraha*, meaning "firmness in a good cause." Gandhi liked the word, but he felt it was not comprehensive, and he changed the word to *Satyagraha*: "Truth (*Satya*) implies love and firmness (*Agraha*) engenders and therefore serves as a synonym for force." *Satyagraha*, then, in Gandhi's thinking is "the Force which is of Truth and Love or nonviolence."[17]

****

In *Stride Toward Freedom* Dr. King wrote at length about his philosophy of nonviolence which was closely influenced by Gandhi's Satyagraha. He argued that nonviolent resistance was "not a method of cowards."[18] He stressed, as Gandhi did, that passive resistance was the wrong term, for it implies "do-nothing."[19] The method is aimed at the enemy—in this case racism, segregation—and not against the people supporting racism and segregation. The method, King felt, accepts hardship and suffering without retaliation. The method is opposed to physical and "internal violence of spirit," for the resister must not hate the opponent. To Dr. King, love was "redemptive good will."

Dr. King read Gandhi while he was in a theological seminary, and earlier, when he was an undergraduate, he had read Thoreau on Civil Disobedience and had been impressed by it. He came to understand that the movement in Montgomery police began to harass blacks in a "get-tough" policy. In the middle of January, 1956, Dr. King left his church office to go home. He picked up passengers going his way[20]—black people no longer using the bus service walked or relied on unofficial taxi

Smuts's Betrayal and the Consequences   151

service run by ministers, teachers, businessmen, unskilled laborers, joined by three white men from air bases who drove passengers on their off hours.

Dr. King noticed that he was being followed by two motorcycle-riding policemen. Dr. King drove slowly and deliberately, following every traffic law. When he stopped to let his passengers out of the car, a policeman came up, saying: "Get out, King; you are under arrest for speeding thirty miles an hour in a twenty-five mile zone." He did get out, was searched, and was placed in a patrol car. The jail was downtown, he thought, incorrectly, but the patrol car was not going in that direction. He was convinced he was being driven to some secluded spot where he would be killed by a mob, with the police claiming that they had been overpowered. Finally, he was relieved to see in the distance a sign, "Montgomery City Jail."[21]

****

Gandhi sat alone before being driven off to jail, but the police in Natal had in the past saved him from a lynch mob. Dr. King, though, knew that police in the Deep South were often complicit in lynchings.

Gandhi wrote a series in English and Gujarati for *Indian Opinion* about his life in jail.[22] He did not show fear in the jail, where his clothes were stripped from him, and he was given dirty clothes formerly worn by Africans. He was not prepared for being housed with African prisoners. The European prison officials put the Indians, Asians, and Africans together, knowing that the Indians and Asians would feel degraded. Gandhi still had stereotypical views of Africans, writing that they were "only one degree removed from the animal." He also complained that the African prisoners yelled throughout the day and into the night.

In his account of his jailing, Gandhi turned to problems with food. European prisoners were fed better than Africans and Asians. The Indian and Chinese political prisoners were not accustomed to mealie pap (maize porridge), for it was difficult to digest.[23] As the number of Indian and Chinese protestors rose, there were some changes in the diet.

Gandhi and other prisoners were allowed to borrow books from the jail library; he brought some books with him and borrowed others. He read works by Carlyle, the lectures by Huxley, essays by Bacon, works by Ruskin, Tolstoy, Plato, and the Bible and the Koran in English. He had plenty of time for reading since he had not been sentenced to hard labor.[24]

****

Dr. King was booked in the jail and placed in a cell with other blacks, including a teacher who had been arrested because of his part in the bus protest. Most of the prisoners were vagrants, drunks, and assorted lawbreakers. White prisoners were in another cell. Dr. King was distressed by the conditions: some men were lying on wooden boards, others on cots with virtually demolished mattresses. The toilet was in the corner without an enclosure, and the odors were powerful. Before he was long there, a friend arrived and Dr. King was released on his own recognizance. Many of his friends were outside the jail, and he once again had the courage he had temporarily lost. He knew that he was not alone in the protest.[25]

****

After Gandhi had been in jail for two weeks, there were stories that it would be possible to reach a negotiated settlement. Then Albert Cartwright, of the *Transvaal Leader* and a man who often supported Indian causes, came to see Gandhi. Cartwright had called on General Jan Christian Smuts, the Transvaal Interior Minister, and carried with him the proposed settlement terms.

General Smuts proposed that Indians should register voluntarily, and that if a majority registered the Transvaal government would repeal the Black Act. The language was unclear about the conditions to be met before the Ordinance was repealed, and Gandhi proposed some alternative language.

Gandhi placed the proposed agreement before his fellow prisoners, who had concerns about the language—they had reason not to trust the government—and they accepted it if General Smuts agreed to the amendment. On

Smuts's Betrayal and the Consequences 153

January 30, 1908, the Superintendent of Police took Gandhi to Pretoria to meet Smuts. The general was clear: he promised that the Asiatic Act would be repealed "as soon as most of you have undergone voluntary registration." Smuts ended by observing that he wanted the matter settled and did not wish "any recurrence of the trouble." Gandhi accepted the terms.

Gandhi was free to go, and the other prisoners would be released the next day. He had no money, but he borrowed train fare from the general's secretary and took the last train that day to Johannesburg.[26]

Gandhi reached Johannesburg, met with community leaders, and called for a special meeting that night on the grounds of a mosque. When the meeting began at midnight, he explained the terms of the agreement, and several there had doubts: "What if General Smuts broke faith with us?" They believed it would be better to have the Act repealed first, followed by the voluntary registration. Gandhi recognized the value of such an argument but felt that the agreement was a compromise, with both sides making concessions.[27]

About one thousand Indians listened to Gandhi's explanation, and only a few had expressed doubts. He was unprepared for the storm that moved in. Mir Alam, a large Pathan, fully six feet tall, with a powerful build, and a Muslim, arose:

"Shall we have to give ten finger-prints under the settlement?"

"Yes and no. My own view of the matter is, that all of us should give digit impressions without the least hesitation. But those, who have any conscientious objection to giving them or think it to be derogatory to their self-respect, will not be obligated to give those impressions."

"What will you do yourself?"

"I have decided to give ten finger-prints. It may not be for me not to give them myself while advising others to do so."

"You were writing a deal about the ten finger-prints. It was you who told us that they were required only from criminals. It was you who said that the struggle centered around finger-prints. How does all that fit in with your attitude today?"

"Even now I fully adhere to everything that I have written before about finger-prints....But circumstances have now changed. I say with all the force at my command, that what would have been a crime against the people yesterday is in the altered circumstances of today the hall-mark of a gentleman. If you require me to salute you by force and if I submit to you, I will have demeaned myself in the eyes of the public and in your eyes as well as in my own. But if I of my own accord salute you as a brother or fellow-man, that evinces my humility and gentlemanliness, and it will be counted to me as righteousness before the Great White Throne. That is how I advise the community to give the finger-prints."

"We have heard that you have betrayed the community and sold it to General Smuts for 15,000 pounds. We will never give the finger-prints nor allow others to do so. I swear with Allah as my witness, that I will kill the man who takes the lead in applying for registration."

"I can understand the feelings of Pathan friends. I am sure that no one else believes me to be capable of selling the community....I will render all possible help to any Pathan or other who wishes to register without giving finger-prints, and I assure him that he will get the certificate all right without violence being done to his conscience. I must confess, however, that I do not like the threat of death which the friend has held out, I also believe that one may not swear to kill another in the name of the Most High. I therefore take it, that it is only in a momentary fit of passion that this friend has taken the oath. However that may be, whether or not he carries out his threat, as the principal party responsible for this settlement and as a servant of the community, it is my clear duty to take the lead in giving finger-prints, and I pray to God that He graciously permit me so to do. Death is the appointed end of all life. To die by the hand of a brother, than by disease or in such other way, cannot be for me a matter of sorrow...."[28]

Gandhi explained in *Satyagraha in South Africa* that Pathans were in small numbers in the Transvaal, fifty members or so. Some had come to the colony during the Boer war. They were brave, and to kill or be killed was truly an ordinary thing for many of them. They often fought among themselves, and in the past Gandhi had served as a peacemaker between warring members. Mir Alam, a businessman, was actually a client of Gandhi's, but Mir Alam was not pacified by the explanation he heard.

Mir Alam's questions and accusation of betrayal did not sway those on the grounds of the mosque, and the compromise was approved.

Gandhi did not get home until two or three the next morning; he had no time for sleep, for at seven he had to be at the jail to meet the 150 or so resisters who were being released. Then there was another meeting to explain the compromise agreement. As days went by, there were additional misunderstandings among the various factions of the Indian community. Gandhi was vague when he mentioned "internal jealousies were again fully in play, as if the differences with the Adversary have been amicably settled, many take to the easy and grateful task of picking holes in the settlement."[29]

What Gandhi did not know at the time was that the nay-sayers were correct in many of their suspicions—but not that Gandhi had been bribed with £15,000.

The Registrar of Asiatics had to prepare new certificates of registration, and on the morning of February 10, 1908, Gandhi set out to register. When Gandhi reached his office at the Satyagraha Association, Mir Alam and some colleagues were standing outside. Gandhi and Mir Alam exchanged brief courtesies, but Gandhi saw that Mir Alam had angry eyes. Gandhi went inside, met the president of the Association and some other friends, and they began walking to the Registration Office, followed by Mir Alam and friends.

When Gandhi and friends were almost to their destination, Mir Alam accosted Gandhi.

"Where are you going?"

"I propose to take out a certificate of registration, giving the ten finger-prints. If you will go with me, I will first get you a certificate, with an impression only of the two thumbs, and then I will take one for myself, giving the finger-prints."

As Gandhi finished that last sentence, he was struck a heavy blow from behind. He fainted with the words *He Rama* (Oh God!) on his lips. Mir Alam and friends continued to strike and kick Gandhi, though his friends tried to come to his aid. The friends were then plummeted. Europeans heard the noise and came to the scene; Mir Alam and friends fled but were caught and held for the police, who arrived and took the assailants into custody.

The bleeding and bruised Gandhi was carried into a nearby office. When he revived, he found the Reverend J. J. Doke, a Baptist minister with wide sympathies for oppressed people, standing over him.

"How do you feel?"

"I am all right, but there is pain in the teeth and the ribs. Where is Mir Alam?"

"He has been arrested along with the rest."

"They should be released."

Mr. Doke offered to take Gandhi to his home, instead of a hospital, to be cared for by the Dokes. Gandhi agreed.

Was the attack on Gandhi a murder attempt? Mir Alam had threatened Gandhi with death, but it appears that the first blow was struck not by Mir Alam but by one of his accomplices who may have been less murderous than Mir Alam.

Smuts's Betrayal and the Consequences

Reverend Doke took Gandhi to his home and called a doctor. In the meantime, Mr. Chamney, the Registrar of Asiatics, arrived. Gandhi said to him:

"I wished to come to your office, give ten finger-prints and take out the first certificate of registration, but God willed it otherwise. However I have now to request you to bring the papers and allow me to register at once. I hope that you will not let any one else register before me."

"Where is the hurry about it? The doctor will be here soon. You please rest yourself and all will be well. I will issue certificates to others but keep your name at the head of the list."

"Not so. I am pledged to take out the first certificate if I am alive and if it is acceptable to God. It is therefore that I insist upon the papers being brought here and now."

Mr. Chamney agreed and returned to his office for the papers. Gandhi then wired the Attorney General that he did not want Mir Alam and companions persecuted and asked that they be discharged. The Attorney General refused and Mr. Alam and friend (undoubtedly the one who hit Gandhi from behind) were sentenced to three months' hard labor.

The doctor came, stitched up Gandhi's wounds, gave him medicine for his ribs, and requested that he remain silent until the stitches on his face were removed. He was to be given liquid food. Gandhi, before resting, addressed a note to the community for publication. He began by announcing that he requested no action be taken against Mir Alam and friends, for they knew not what they were doing. He continued:

"Seeing that the assault was committed by a Musalman or Musalmans, the Hindus might probably feel hurt. If so, they would not put themselves in the wrong before the world and their Maker. Rather let the blood spilt today cement the two communities indissolubly—such is my heartfelt prayer. May God grant it." Gandhi's plea for communal unity was a long-standing wish of his, but the communities were being pulled apart.[30]

The Dokes took excellent care of Gandhi, who had known Mr. Doke for a short time—since December 1907, when he called on Gandhi in his office. Gandhi incorrectly though, seeing "Reverend" before his name, thought the minister had come to convert him to Christianity or to ask him to give up the struggle. Gandhi was wrong. Doke had been following the protest movement in the newspapers and said, "Please consider me as your friend in this struggle. I consider it my religious duty to render you such help as I can." Over the following months, Doke became a part of Gandhi's inner circle.

Gandhi stayed with the Dokes for about ten days. Some of the Dokes' neighbors were distressed that they were caring for a man of color, but the Dokes did not falter. Rev. Doke told Gandhi that many Europeans were in silent sympathy with the tribulation of Indians. Gandhi hoped for such sympathy when Europeans saw the suffering of nonviolent Indians.[31]

Once Gandhi recovered from his injuries, he left the Transvaal to see his family at Phoenix settlement, to discuss the agreement to register, and to attend to *Indian Opinion* affairs. After his arrival, he called a meeting of Indians in Durban at 8 o'clock p.m. As the session was ending, a Pathan rushed upon the stage carrying a large stick. Some of those on the stage surrounded Gandhi to keep him from harm, and Mr. Rustomji rushed to the police station to alert Superintendent Alexander, who once again used his men to protect Gandhi.[32]

The next day, Gandhi met with Pathans living in Durban, but his attempts to placate them failed. They felt that he had betrayed the Indian community, and nothing Gandhi could say changed their opinion.

By early May, 1908, 8,700 Indians had voluntarily registered, more than half the population. The community could expect the Black Act to be repealed, as agreed to by General Smuts, then the most powerful man in the Transvaal government. Instead of repeal, Smuts introduced more anti-Indian legislation. His explanation was that he could not implement his promise to Gandhi because Europeans were opposed.[33] Smuts had breached the agreement, but Gandhi did not demonize the general. Some in the Indian community accused Gandhi of being easily mislead, and to that charge he asserted that what seemed to be credulity was in fact trust.[34] The racist European community, though, had outwitted Gandhi.

Europeans then began to apply economic pressure against well-known Satyagrahis such as A. M. Kachhalia, the merchant. He owed money to European firms, and the Transvaal government, directly or indirectly, urged the creditors to demand immediate payment. Kachhalia could not meet that call, but his balance sheet showed that he was solvent. He was forced into bankruptcy, and his European creditors later received a full 20 shillings on the pound. It was a double win for the European businessmen—they shamed a dissident and forcing Kachhalia out of business meant their own businesses could expand. According to Gandhi, Kachhalia was not broken by this despicable act of Europeans against him. He wore the badge of failure with pride, for he was an innocent party.[35]

****

In Montgomery, Alabama, during the bus boycott, some blacks did lose their jobs. After her arrest, Rosa Parks was fired from the department store where she was a seamstress. Boycotting domestics could not be intimidated by economic threats. Said one black maid: "Pooh! My white lady ain't going to get down and mop that kitchen floor. I know that."[36]

Juliette Morgan, a white librarian in Montgomery, wrote the *Advertiser*, "The Negroes of Montgomery seem to have taken a lesson from Gandhi—and our own Thoreau, who influenced Gandhi. Their own task is greater than Gandhi's, however, for they have greater prejudice to overcome. One feels that history is being made in Montgomery these days, the most important in her career. It is hard to imagine a soul so dead, a heart so hard, a vision so blinded and provincial as not to be moved with admiration at the quiet dignity, discipline and dedication with which the Negroes have conducted their boycott." For this letter, Juliette Morgan lost her job and was condemned by white society. An outcast, she took her own life.[37] Dr. King and other boycott leaders saw the connections between the boycott, Gandhi and Thoreau.

Dr. King wrote that the name of Mahatma Gandhi became well known in Montgomery and that nonviolent resistance was the technique being used in the protest: "Christ furnished the spirit and motivation, while Gandhi furnished the method."[38]

Gandhi had to deal with the antagonisms between Hindus and Muslims. Dr. King found that the various faiths in the black community worked together,[39] to be joined later by some white religious groups. Gandhi did have Indian Opinion to spread the word about Indian affairs in South Africa. There were few large-circulation African American newspapers, and black churches were pivotal in providing information about meetings and demonstrations, their time and place, and general information about the protests.

****

Faced with the bad faith of General Smuts, the Satyagraha Association took another approach to defiance. A large cauldron was placed on the grounds of a mosque in Johannesburg. At 4 p.m. on August 16, 1908, the Association called a meeting to protest the Asiatic bill. Indians had requested a repeal of the racist act, but the government sent a telegram that it would not do so. About 2,000 certificates had been placed in the pot. Mir Alam was present and told the audience that he had been wrong to assault Gandhi. Gandhi responded that he held no resentment. Gandhi assured the huge crowd present that anyone who wanted his certificate back could have it without question or censure. No one responded.

Parafin (kerosene) was poured over the certificates, and they were set afire. Those present then rose to their feet and continually cheered while the hated certificates burned. Now more than 2,000 Indians were civil disobedients, subject to jailing.[40]

Gandhi was influenced by several sources when he oversaw the burning of the certificates. He would have known from his reading of Salt's biog-

Smuts's Betrayal and the Consequences 161

raphy of Thoreau that Thoreau read "Slavery in Massachusetts" at an anti-slavery meeting in Framingham, Massachusetts, on July 4, 1854. At that meeting, William Lloyd Garrison, in a dramatic act, burned the Constitution of the United States because it legitimized slavery.

The Johannesburg reporter for *The Daily Mail* of London sent a story about the fiery meeting, comparing the act of Indians to that of the Boston Tea Party. Gandhi found some justice in the comparison but pointed out in America at the time of the Tea Party there were thousands of strong Europeans facing the British Empire. In the Transvaal, there were 13,000 Indians without weapons. He believed, "The Indians' only weapon was a faith in the righteousness of their own cause and in God."

The certificates, purified in the fire, had ceased to be. Indians had twisted the tail of the British lion; they expected roars and then arrests.

Notes

1. Rajmohan Gandhi, *Mohandas*, pp. 125–27; Gandhi, *Satyagraha in South Africa*, pp. 182–93.
2. Gandhi, *Satyagraha in South Africa*, p. 186.
3. Martin Green, *Gandhi*, p. 224; James D. Hunt, *Gandhi in London*, pp. 101–104.
4. Gandhi, *Satyagraha in South Africa*, p. 189.
5. Ibid., pp.197–98; Gandhi, Collected Works, 6:430–31.
6. Gandhi, *Satyagraha in South Africa*, pp. 210–14; Rajmohan Gandhi, *Mohandas*, p. 129.
7. Gandhi, Collected Works, 7:55,202.
8. Ibid., 7:55, 202.
9. Hendrick, *Henry Salt*, p. 112.
10. Gandhi, Collected Works, 7:211–12.
11. Ibid., 7:217–18.
12. Ibid., 7:230.
13. Ibid., 7:304–305.
14. Ibid., 7:304–305.
15. Hendrick, *Henry Salt*, p. 112.
16. Thoreau, Walden, the first page of the "Sounds" chapter.
17. Gandhi, *Satyagraha in South Africa*, pp. 173–81; Rajmohan Gandhi, *Mohandas*, p. 129.
18. King, *Stride Toward Freedom*, pp. 51, 101–7.
19. Ibid., p. 102.
20. Ibid., pp. 126–27.
21. King, *Stride Toward Freedom*, pp. 127–29; Oates, *Let the Trumpet Sound*, pp. 82–83.
22. Gandhi wrote about his first experiences in jail in *Collected Works of Mahatma Gandhi*, 8:119–21, 134–36, 139–42, 152–55.
23. Gandhi, *Satyagraha in South Africa*, pp. 225–37;Gandhi, *Collected Works*, 8:120.
24. Gandhi, *Collected Works*, 8:159.
25. King, *Stride Toward Freedom*, pp. 129–31.
26. Gandhi, *Satyagraha in South Africa*, pp. 239–43.
27. Ibid., pp. 244–45.

28. Ibid., pp. 249–52. Mir Alam is not identified by name in *Satyagraha in South Africa* but by Rajmohan Gandhi, *Mohandas*, p. 132.
29. Gandhi, *Satyagraha in South Africa*, pp. 255–65.
30. Ibid., pp. 261–62.
31. Ibid., pp. 259–67.
32. Ibid., pp. 283–85
33. Rajmohan Gandhi, *Mohandas*, p.135.
34. Gandhi, *Satyagraha in South Africa*, pp. 293–94.
35. Ibid., pp. 295–301.
36. Oates, *Let the Trumpet Sound*, p. 73.
37. Ibid., pp. 73–74.
38. King, *Stride Toward Freedom*, p. 85.
39. Ibid., pp. 85–86.
40. Gandhi, *Satyagraha in South Africa*, p.310–13.

CHAPTER X

THE SATYAGRAHA MOVEMENT SAVED BY JUSTICE SEARLE

The weeks after the burning of certificates were difficult for Gandhi and the Satyagraha movement. Many Indian business men did not approve of the burning. Others were wary of going to jail. The government made a few arrested but resisted mass imprisonment for a time. Those arrested seem to have been the true believers in the nonviolent movement.

Gandhi was arrested on October 7, 1908, as he returned to the Transvaal after a visit to Natal. He had no registration certificate, for it had been burned. He was sentenced to two months of hard labor. During this jailing episode, he faced a harsher government, one now actively hoping to break his spirit. He and fellow prisoners broke up rocks, dug pits and trenches, and other menial tasks.[1]

Gandhi was actually in danger once he was transferred to the Johannesburg jail to testify in another trial. His arms manacled and wearing convict garb, he was marched through the streets, a leading barrister now a convicted criminal.[2] He was a political prisoner, and the government though his spirit could be broken, but Gandhi was sustained by knowledge of the suffragettes in England who were mistreated in jail and also by Thoreau's going to jail for a principle.

In that jail, he was housed with hardened criminals. Two of the prisoners—a Chinese and a Kaffir—were apparently threatening to rape him; they "exchanged obscene jokes, uncovering each other's genitals."[3] Gandhi stayed awake that night, fearful of an assault that did not come, reciting lines from the *Gita*.

Gandhi was attacked in the prison toilet. Sitting in an open stall, Gandhi was lifted up by "a strong, heavily-built fearful-looking Native" who wanted that particular seat. Gandhi saved himself by catching onto a door frame and did not hit the floor.[4] The government knew Gandhi was vulnerable when he was housed with hardened criminals.

****

In Atlanta, Dr. King was arrested for a traffic violation. He recognized immediately how much danger he was in, even before he reached jail. At 3 o'clock in the morning, he was taken for a long ride to Reidsville State Prison. He was treated like a common prisoner: chained, with his legs tied to the floor. His captors talked among themselves during the long ride, and he was in anguish, for he could only speculate on what was going to happen to him.[5] Prisoners in Georgia opposed to segregation had reason to fear when they were in the captivity of certain police officers.

****

These experiences in jail and the fierce hostility to Indians made Gandhi think of his death. On January 29, 1909, from the Volksrust jail, he wrote: "My enthusiasm is such that I may have to meet death in South Africa at the hands of my own countrymen."[6] His death was as predicted, assassinated by his own countryman, as was Dr. King.

****

Frequently in danger from violent mobs, Dr. King often spoke of his death. During his last speech he ever made, in Memphis, Tennessee, on April 3, 1968, he said: "I've been to the mountain top," using the story of Moses. "I

The Satyagraha Movement Saved by Justice Searle 167

just want to do God's will. And He's allowed me to go up to the mountain. And I've looked over, and I've seen the promised land. I may not get there with you. But I want you to know tonight, that we, as a people, will get to the promised land."[7]

****

While in prison, Gandhi learned that wife was hemorrhaging and seriously ill. He did not pay his fine and go to her bedside. Instead he wrote a chilling letter: "I love you so dearly that even if you are dead, you will be alive to me. Your soul is deathless. I repeat what I have frequently told you and assure you that if you do succumb to your illness, I will not marry again. ...If you die, even that death of yours will be a sacrifice to the cause of Satyagraha. My struggle is not entirely political. It is religious and therefore quite pure. It does not matter much whether one dies in it or lives."[8]

He demonstrated his love in a strange way. When he came from jail, he waited two weeks before going to her, even though she remained ill. Gandhi and Mrs. Gandhi had continued to be far apart in their views. Harilal, their older son, had returned to South Africa with his wife and child and was still distressed that his father would not support his goal of a higher education. Mrs. Gandhi supported her son. Gandhi had other pressing concerns: the Satyagraha movement, now being actively punished by the government.

The Transvaal government began to deport to India those Indians without certificates. Most had been born in South Africa and had never lived in India. These deportations helped the Transvaal government, for a considerable number of Indians left the Satyagraha movement, hoping to find a way to stay where they were.

Intense agitation of these cruel deportations did force the government to halt them, but that victory was hardly a victory. The government just looked for other ways to harass Indians.[9]

Leaders of South Africa's Europeans in 1909 were in London working to merge the four colonies into the Union of South Africa. Indians understood that unified colonies would make the lives of Indians there even more difficult or even impossible. The doomed solution of the Indians: send a delegation to London to seek help from the British government.

Gandhi and Haji Habib were chosen as the delegation; they left in June and arrived on July 10, 1909, for a stay of four months. Again, Gandhi was busy talking to government leaders and journalists, everyone and anyone who might help. General Botha, in London, sent a message. He would make minor concession, but he would not repeal the Asiatic Act or make changes in the Immigrants Restriction Act which barred educated Indians. He would not remove the color bar. The trip to London was a failure. The British government would not intervene to assist Indians. The Satyagraha movement had to continue.[10]

On the voyage back to South Africa Gandhi wrote one of his most controversial texts. For years, he had been speaking about failures in Western civilization. In his pamphlet, *Indian Home Rule or Hind Swaraj* he attacked a corrupt, decadent Western civilization, not worthy of support. He believed that Indians were indeed in a state of slavery, and his cry was for Home Rule in India.

The text was aimed for Indians in India. Although there were praiseworthy parts of this work, he often used unconvincing arguments in his attack on Western civilization and idealized a much earlier life in his country. A Puritan in many ways, he romanticized an early, moral life in his country of birth but produced no concept of what a free India would be like. Would the princes remain in power? Would there be an elected president? Would Hindus, Muslims, Parsis, and other religions unite to form a new government? What would be the fate of untouchables in this new society? Would the government outlaw industrialism? medicine?

Gandhi attacked industrial developments, supported by the Raj. The Raj used the railroad as an important part of their power structure, and he argued that railroads were responsible for the bubonic plague. Without this new mode of rapid transportation, the populace would not move from place to place and spread this plague. Gandhi wanted to recreate a pre-industrial society.

Gandhi had once wanted to become a physician, but his views changed. In the pamphlet, he argued that the business of doctors was to rid the body of diseases: A person overeats and has indigestion. The doctor gives him effective medicine and the indigestion goes away. The person overeats again. "The doctor," Gandhi argued, "intervened and helped me to indulge myself. My body thereby certainly felt more at ease but my mind became weakened."[11] The argument is a weak one and does not support his view that physicians should give up their practice and "mend souls."[12] Modern medicine is deeply troubled, and Gandhi, with more thought and information, could have been compelling.

Gandhi also urged attorneys to give up their professions and "take up a handloom."[13] Within a few years, Gandhi in India turned to spinning, having given up the practice of law. Many Americans would agree with Gandhi and abhor that profession.

He wanted the wealthy man to give his money to establish handlooms and thus provide local cloth for India instead of importing it from England. This boycott was successful.

He did urge nonviolent protest and the acceptance of suffering while following higher laws and disobeying the rule of the Raj. These were qualities which have made Gandhi internationally famous, and his anti-industrial, anti-machinery, anti-lawyer, anti-doctor statements are now forgotten or reinterpreted.

****

The civil rights movement under Dr. King rejected the anti-education, anti-industrial stances of Gandhi. Dr. King wanted equal desegregated educational opportunities for African Americans, as well as job opportunities for all. He shared with Gandhi a commitment to the poor and dispossessed.

****

In addition, Gandhi urged his followers devoted to India to be chaste: "A man who is unchaste loses stamina, becomes emasculated and cowardly." He urged married couples to refrain from sexual activity unless they wished progeny, but, he wrote "a passive resister has to avoid even that very limited indulgence because he can have no desire for progeny."[14] Gandhi set standards for his Satyagraha followers that forced them to lie about their sexual life or become chaste. Later civil disobedience movements in many parts of the world have ignored Gandhi's call for chastity.

Indian Home Rule or Hind Swaraj, imperfect as it is, did propose some ways to be used by Indians to free their country from the British rulers. Naturally, the Raj banned it in India.

During his time in London in 1909, Gandhi wrote Tolstoy a long letter on October 1 about the problems Indians were facing in South Africa. Tolstoy responded on October 7, 1909: "May God help all our dear brothers and co-workers in the Transvaal. This fight between gentleness and brutality between humility and love on one side, and conceit and violence on the other, makes itself ever more strongly felt here to us also—especially in the sharp conflicts between religious obligations and the laws of the State—expressed by the conscientious objection to render military service."[15]

On October 19, 1909, Gandhi responded, sending a copy of Reverend J. J. Doke's biography titled *M. K. Gandhi: An Indian Patriot in South Africa*. Rev. Doke was one of the few Protestant ministers who looked with favor on Gandhi, who took him into his home to recover from a brutal attack, and who worked for the Satyagraha movement. From reading this clearly-written pamphlet of 103 pages, it is obvious that Doke conducted many interviews with Gandhi, and the tone and content are much like Gandhi's *Autobiography*.[16] Missing, though, are references to his problems with his wife and sons and with his sexuality. The Doke biography of Gandhi was a good introduction to Gandhi's nonviolence for readers and

The Satyagraha Movement Saved by Justice Searle 171

for Tolstoy. On October 1 Gandhi sent Tolstoy an account of nonviolence movement and Doke's book.

Gandhi wrote Tolstoy on November 10, 1909, asking the famous Russian dissident to use his influence to advertise the South African movement, that is, if he were satisfied by the facts set forth in Doke's pamphlet. Gandhi continued: "In my opinion, this struggle of the Indians in the Transvaal is the greatest of modern times, inasmuch as it has been idealized both as to the goal as also to the methods adopted to reach the goal. I am not aware of a struggle in which the participators are not to derive any personal advantage at the end of it and in which 50 per cent of the persons affected have undergone great suffering and trial for the sake of a principle."[17]

Gandhi wanted Tolstoy to pass the torch to him.

With the mission to London a failure, Gandhi realized that the jailing of Indians would continue, even intensify. What to do with the families of these jailed men? They could not easily be sent to Phoenix Farm three hundred miles away from Johannesburg. Mrs. Gandhi and three of their sons were living at Phoenix, and Gandhi kept his distance from them. Harilal was jailed, unhappily believing that his father had applied undue pressure to get him to join the Satyagraha movement.

In the early days of the jailings, families were given small monthly allowances in cash for their support. Funds for these payments were always in short supply. Gandhi had largely given up his profitable law practice and did not have personal funds to contribute. There were several surprises: Gandhi's friend Gokhale announced that the industrialist Tata had given Rupees 25,000 to the movement, and soon afterwards several Indian princes donated funds. Then Hermann Kallenbach, the wealthy architect, bought on May 30, 1910, a thousand acre, fertile farm twenty miles from Johannesburg. The farm had one house on it and many orange, apricot, and plum trees. Kallenbach allowed the families to use the farm without payment. He oversaw the building of simple houses on the property. A name was chosen: Tolstoy Farm.

Gandhi had men and women housed in different units, widely separated. Kallenbach was in residence, and a house was built for him. There was also a school, a workshop for carpentry and shoemaking. Gandhi wanted to make the farm as self-sufficient as possible. The diet was vegetarian. Gandhi wrote that had Christians or Muslims requested meat, their wishes would have been met. This is undoubtedly true, for he respected other religions and their traditions, but he undoubtedly had some private conversations to make certain that all at Tolstoy Farm would eat fruits and vegetables only.

The simple life there, indebted as it was to Thoreau, was put into place on a large scale. All washed their own kitchen utensils; all had chores, including the children. All ate together in a single line. Tobacco and alcohol were forbidden.

Gandhi had the insights of a public health nurse or physician. Tolstoy Farm was kept clean. Rubbish was buried. Waste water was collected and used to water trees. Nightsoil was buried in a pit and covered with earth each day to keep flies from gathering.

Great efforts were made to make the farm self-sufficient. Kallenbach went to the Trappists to learn sandal making and taught Gandhi. Bread was made from ground whole wheat. Peanuts were roasted and ground to make peanut butter. Oranges were used to make marmalade. When members of the farm went into Johannesburg they took food with them. Most walked to Johannesburg and then back, but if longer travel was necessary, the person went by train third class.[18]

Gandhi and Kallenbach were the teachers. Gandhi wanted the children to become familiar with Hindu, Muslim, Christian texts. He seems to have developed a comparative religion curriculum. His intention was to save children from intolerance and "to view one another's religions and customs with a large-hearted charity."[19] He did wish the children to have instruction in their own language, stressing that English was not the only language worth speaking and writing.

Gandhi was a taskmaster, an authoritarian in charge of Tolstoy Farm. In general, utopian experiments such as this one, stressing the simple life and communal living, had an extended life only if they had a strong leader.

Gandhi was blissfully unaware of some elements of human conduct. As an experiment, he treated the children as if they were in the Garden of Eden, before the fall. Boys and girls, presumably without clothes, bathed together. Gandhi was present: "My eye always followed the girls as a mother's eye would follow a daughter."[20] He was struggling to remain asexual, but his sentence reveals more than he intended.

At night, Gandhi and the children slept on an open veranda. Their beds were around his, separated by about three feet. Gandhi indicated that no sexual activity could have taken place because he was a light sleeper. He was apparently unaware or unwilling to admit the wiles of adolescents.

An incident when the young people were bathing together became a major moral problem for Gandhi. One day some of the boys made fun of two girls. Gandhi's tortured account of his reaction reveals another aspect of his repressed sexuality: "I remonstrated with the young men, but that was not enough. I wished the two girls to have some sign on their person as a warning to every young man that no evil eye might be cast upon them, and as a lesson to every girl that no one dare assail their purity." He spent a sleepless night before coming to a solution: shave off the long hair of the girls. The older women objected, to no avail; the two girls were reluctant, but they were persuaded by Gandhi to agree. He cut their hair, but the boys were not so marked. He was seemingly unaware of the psychological damage he had done and said that the girls did not lose, they gained. He did not understand adolescent boys struggling with their sexuality, either: "I hope the young men still remember this incident end keep their eye from sin."[21]

Harilal, Gandhi's first-born son, in the years 1908–1911 served six terms in jail for his civil disobedience. He continued to be angry with his father for not sending him to England for advanced education. He had studied in India but had not completed his work, and there is some indication that he was, even in his early 20s, something of a wastrel, given to gambling. His continuing problems with his father contributed, in part, to his personal excesses and failures.

Harilal sent his wife and daughter back to India, and then he disappeared without telling his father of his plans to rejoin his wife. Kallenbach found he was in Mozambique, rushed there, and brought Harilal back to Johannesburg. Father and son talked an entire night, but the differences remained. The next day, May 17, 1911, Harilal left for India with Gandhi at the station asking for forgiveness and he kissed his son.[22] Mrs. Gandhi and the younger sons supported Harilal.

Gandhi was often harsh in his comments, as in this letter to Laxmidas on July 27, 1906: "It is well if Harilal is married; it is also well if he is not. For the present at any rate I have ceased to think of him as a son."[23] The father-son differences continued year after year.

At Tolstoy Farm Gandhi continued to work as physician, and, as in the past, he preferred nature cures. An ancient man from North India suffered from asthma. Gandhi had him stop smoking and fast for an entire day. At noon Gandhi gave him a Kuhne bath in the sun, and the man was given a restricted diet. He failed to get better, but Gandhi discovered he was secretly smoking. Once the old man stopped smoking, he improved and was then well, or so Gandhi declared.

For a child diagnosed with typhoid, Gandhi gave the patient nothing the first day, then half a banana mashed with olive oil and orange juice. At night he put a cold mud pack on the child's stomach. The treatment was successful, but Gandhi casts some doubt on his medical skill by reporting that it was possible that the doctor's diagnosis was wrong and the child did not have typhoid.[24]

The Satyagraha Movement Saved by Justice Searle   175

Gandhi's most intense relationship at this time was with Kallenbach.[25] At the same time, and over a period of years, Polak was also vying for Gandhi's love and affection. Kallenbach and Polak were successful in emotionally bonding with Gandhi, but Mrs. Gandhi and Harilal were not usually so fortunate.

Gokhale, Gandhi's mentor, came to South Africa to study the conditions of Indians, then much in the news in India and England. He arrived in Cape Town on October 22, 1912. Both government officials and Indian groups greeted him with great enthusiasm. Gandhi served him as secretary and informant. Much of the tour was ceremonial, but Gokhale did have a two hour meeting with the two most important leaders in South Africa —Botha and Smuts. Gandhi had often clashed with these South African officials and wisely did not attend the meeting, but he did provide Gokhale with important background material about the injustices Indians faced. Gokhale thought the meeting was productive. He assured Gandhi that the major problems were settled: The Black Act will be repealed. The racial bar will be removed from the emigration law. The £3 tax will be abolished.

Gandhi responded: "I doubt it very much. You do not know the ministers as I do. Being an optimist myself, I love your optimism, but having suffered frequent disappointments, I am not as hopeful in the matter as you are....The promise given to you will serve as a proof of the justice of our demands and will redouble our fighting spirit if it comes to fighting after all."[26]

Gokhale wanted Gandhi to return to India within a year to work on the massive problems in that country. Gandhi was hesitant, for he believed that Botha and Smuts would not make major concessions. He believed many more would go to jail in South Africa before Indians were given the rights they possessed as citizens of the British Empire.

Gandhi was soon to learn that his analysis was correct. Before the intentions of the government became clear, Gandhi and Kallenbach accompanied Gokhale to Zanzibar (Gokhale was returning to India) and had long discussions about the visit. Gokhale was impressed with Sonja Schlesin and praised her "purity, single-minded devotion to work and great determination." He recognized her sacrifices to the Indian cause, made without any expectation of reward. Her ability and energy was "a priceless"[27] asset to the Satyagraha movement. Gokhale's praise was merited. She alone in Gandhi's inner circle was always willing to speak the truth, as she saw it, to Gandhi. Polak would speak up at times, but not consistently. Kallenbach followed Gandhi's wishes. The personality cult around Gandhi was beginning to develop, but Sonja Schlesin, a true believer in the movement, was independent. Unfortunately, she did not write her memoirs. After Gandhi departed South Africa in 1914, she became a headmistress at a school for girls. She would have been a great asset had she, instead, gone to India to work for Indian home rule there.

Gokhale had been deceived. General Smuts from his seat in the Union Parliament announced that Europeans in Natal wished to retain the £3 tax, and the Government would not press for its removal. Gokhale was firm; he declared that concessions had been made during the two hour meeting with Smuts and Botha. The Government argued that Gokhale had misunderstood and that the possibilities of repeal of the hated act had merely been discussed. What Gokhale had seen as a pledge had been broken. Gandhi recognized that the struggle had to continue.

Gandhi faced a new problem. The Government's brutal treatment of jailed Sataygraha followers caused many Indians to leave the movement. Gandhi had few followers left. It looked as if the Government would win the struggle. Gokhale asked Gandhi for the maximum and minimum strength of the "army of peace." The response: 65 or 66 was the highest number Gandhi could count on and 16 was the lowest. Such an army could not fill the jails as had been done during the jailings of 1908–1909 when 3,000 to 4,000 Indians were imprisoned.[28]

Gandhi, like Thoreau, would act alone if necessary. He began making plans for a long struggle. The few remaining inhabitants at Tolstoy Farm were moved to the Phoenix settlement to save money.

The Satyagraha Movement Saved by Justice Searle

Startlingly, a court ruling energized the weakened Satyagraha movement. Mr. Justice Searle of the Cape Supreme Court ruled that marriages of Indians were invalid unless celebrated according to Christian rites and registered with the "Registrar of Marriages." As Gandhi wrote: "There is no law for the registration of ordinary marriages in India, and the religious ceremony suffices to confer validity upon them."[29] With his ruling, Indian wives became concubines and children were no longer legitimate and could not inherit. Indian men and women were appalled both in South Africa and India, and it is likely that some European women felt sympathy and compassion for Indian women and their children.

Indian women, including Mrs. Gandhi, wanted to join the struggle and did so. Male Indian shopkeepers and businessmen (mostly Muslims) who had drifted away or who had always kept clear of the movement were now drawn to it.

****

The Dred Scott decision in the United States and Justice Searle's ruling shared many similarities. Dred Scott, a Missouri slave, had been taken by his "owner" into free territory. Dred Scott then sued, requesting his freedom, for he had been in an area where slavery was forbidden. Chief Justice Roger Taney, member of a slaveholding family, ruled in a 7–2 1857 decision that Scott had no standing to sue in a federal court because blacks were not citizens and had no rights. He wrote for the majority: "They had for more than a century before been regarded as beings of an inferior order; and altogether unfit to associate with the white race, either in social or political relations; and so far inferior that they had no rights which the white man was bound to respect: and that the negro might justly and lawfully be reduced to slavery for his benefit."[30]

****

The Taney ruling was a victory for the pro-slavery forces in the United States, but abolitionists and others were appalled by the inhumane finding, were committed to ending slavery, and the anti-slavery movement grew. Justice Searle's ruling revitalized the Satyagraha movement and Gandhi began to receive more recruits. The next phase of the movement was ready to begin.

Notes

1. Rajmohan Gandhi, *Mohandas*, p. 137.
2. Ibid., p. 137.
3. Gandhi, *Collected Works*, 9:256; Rajmohan Gandhi, *Mohandas*, p. 137.
4. Gandhi, *Collected Works*, 9:270.
5. Martin Luther King, Jr., *Autobiography*, p. 147.
6. Robert Payne, *Life and Death of Mahatma Gandhi*, pp. 192–93; Gandhi, *Collected Works*, 9:175.
7. Martin Luther King, Jr., *Autobiography*, p. 365.
8. Payne, *Life and Death of Mahatma Gandhi*, pp. 192–93; Gandhi, *Collected Works*, 9:106.
9. Gandhi, *Satyagraha in South Africa*, pp. 338–46.
10. Ibid., pp. 347–53.
11. Gandhi, *Indian Home Rule, or Hind Swaraj*, Madras: G. A. Nateson & Co., 6th ed.. n.d. p. 52.
12. Ibid., p. 107.
13. Ibid., p. 106.
14. Ibid., p. 85.
15. Kalindas Nag, *Tolstoy and Gandhi*, p. 63.
16. I used the first Indian edition of Joseph J. Doke, *M.K. Gandhi: An Indian Patriot in South Africa*. Madras: G. A. Nateson & Co., n.d.
17. Nag, *Tolstoy and Gandhi*, pp. 64–65.
18. Gandhi describes Tolstoy Farm in *Satyagraha in South Africa*, pp. 354–93.
19. Ibid., p. 369.
20. Ibid., p. 372.
21. Ibid., pp. 373–74.
22. The best discussion of Harilal's leaving is in Rajmohan Gandhi, *Mohandas*, pp. 162–64.
23. Gandhi, *Collected Works*, 5:335.
24. Gandhi, *Satyagraha in South Africa*, pp. 388–90.
25. Lelyveld, *Great Soul*, pp. 95–97.
26. Gandhi, *Satyagraha in South Africa*, p. 408.
27. Ibid., p. 275.
28. Ibid., pp. 412–18; the "army of peace" is from p. 416; Rajmohan Gandhi, *Mohandas*, p. 139.

29. Gandhi, *Satyagraha in South Africa*, p. 419.
30. Hine, Hine, and Harrold, *The African–American Odyssey*, p. 216.

Chapter XI

Nonviolence Succeeded but Racism Remained

By 1913 most of Gandhi's supporters had dwindled away. Hindu and Muslim merchants were not enthusiastic about going to jail. Indentured and ex-endured Indians (mostly Hindu) were struggling to exist in a hostile environment and had not been organized and radicalized, At most, Gandhi had 66 supporters and possibly only 16.

Gandhi recognized that he was in need of an increase in the number of Satyagrahis. Mr. Justice Searle of the Cape Supreme Court provided Gandhi with a dramatic issue by nullifying all marriages celebrated according to Hindu, Muslim, and Zoroastrian rites, thereby making the wives concubines and the children illegitimate. Gandhi used the publicity in England and the Indian sub-continent to build support for the movement. South African officials in their hatred for Indians and their desire for a European-dominated society were attacking women and children. Mr. Justice Searle had committed a Himalayan blunder, and Gandhi began to use it for his own advantage.

Gandhi also began to make use of women in the movement; he already had Sonja Schlesin working in the Indian rights campaign.

Lack of settlers meant that Tolstoy Farm had to be closed, and Gandhi went to Phoenix to recruit active resisters. Sixteen members there, with four women including Mrs. Gandhi, decided to be an invading party courting arrest in the Transvaal. Once these ferocious protestors entered the Transvaal, they were arrested. They refused to identify themselves when arrested and only made their names known in court. They were sentenced on September 23, 1913, to ninety days in prison, with hard labor. The women were especially subjected to harsh treatment and given inadequate or inappropriate food. Gandhi used this mistreatment to advantage, for stories about Indian women in jail with common criminals caused an outcry in India itself.

A group of Indian women in the Transvaal had courted arrest by entering Natal without a permit. At first, the Natal government ignored them, and the women made a strategic move, something Gandhi himself had not planned. They went to Newcastle to work among the thousands of Indians working in the coal mines. These ill-paid miners were subject to the £3 tax, which greatly decreased their meager incomes. The women organized them, and the miners went on strike.[1]

This was an audacious activity of the Indian women and led to the final phase of Gandhi's activities in South Africa.

****

In the spring of 1963, Dr. King and his staff made the decision to begin using children in the protest movement. Staff members visited high schools and colleges, inviting students to attend meetings on nonviolence in churches, and a large number of them responded. These young people lived in segregated Birmingham, Alabama, and attended segregated schools and colleges. They wanted segregation to end. The young protesters were formed into a "Children's Crusade," which began May 2 and continued until May 7.

Nonviolence Succeeded but Racism Remained 183

The Police Commissioner of Birmingham, Eugene ("Bull") Connor, an ardent segregationist, was determined to stop the planned march of the children. The marchers came to a barricade erected by the police; they were chanting "we want freedom!" The children refused to return to the church and Connor first ordered the police to turn the fire hoses on them, knocking them down or into buildings and driving them back into the nearby park. Some African Americans, failing to follow nonviolence practice, threw bricks at Connor's forces. The Police Commissioner then turned the fierce police dogs on the children, who fled in fear. Connor sneered, "Look at those niggers run."

Hundreds of young demonstrators went to jail that day; more than a thousand were jailed during the crusade.

Reporters filed stories about what they had seen, and perhaps more importantly, photographers captured the scenes of children downed by water hoses and then being attacked by dogs. The stories end photographs went around the world. As Dr. King wrote, "The moral conscience of the nation was stirred." Using the children was a calculated risk Dr. King took.[2]

****

The government could no longer ignore the Indian women, and they were arrested and sentenced to three months of prison. Again the stories reached India and the South African government was put into an unfavorable light.

The striking miners faced retribution; they lived in company towns. The owners turned off the lights and gas and threw out the personal property of the miners.

Before the women were arrested, they were staying with Mr. D. Lazarus, a Christian Tamilian, who lived in a small house on a small plot of ground. Mr. Lazarus was a member of a family of indentured laborers and understood the impact of the £3 tax on Indian workers. Gandhi also stayed with Mr. Lazarus. At an earlier time, he had stayed with Indian merchants, but to do so during the strike would invite financial ruin on those merchants, for Europeans would withdraw their business from those sympathetic to the strikers.[3]

Gandhi urged the strikers to leave their houses and possessions, taking only their clothes, and march away. But how would Gandhi take care of them? At first, the strikers began congregating on Mr. Lazarus's farm, but he was not a rich man and could not feed hundreds of people who came with no possessions except their clothes end blankets.

Gandhi planned a march from near Newcastle to the Transvaal border (35 miles), where they might be arrested and put in prison; this would be a disaster for the government to deal with mass arrests, then on to Johannesburg (125 miles) and from there to Tolstoy Farm (22 miles).[4]

Gandhi thought there were from 5,000 to 6,000 marchers, but that number is probably too large. Some of the strikers brought their wives and children with them. There was no shelter for this crowd, but the weather was pleasant, warm and sunny.

Gandhi did not have money to feed the strikers, but the local traders brought cooking utensils, rice and *dal*, vegetables, and condiments. Many of these traders must have acted surreptitiously, for it was dangerous for Europeans to know about their sympathies.[5]

In his chapter "A Stream of Labourers" in *Satyagraha in South Africa* about organizing the march starting from Newcastle, Gandhi made a remarkable concession about the Indians getting ready to march: "Some of them had been to jail for criminal offences such as murder, theft or adultery. But I did not consider myself fit to sit in judgment over the morality of the strikers. It would have been silly for me to attempt at distinguishing between the goats and the sheep. My business was only to conduct the strike, which could not be mixed up with any other reforming activity. I was indeed bound to see that the rules of morality were observed in the camp, but it was not for me to inquire into the antecedents of each striker."[6] In this special case, vital to the recently floundering, now energized Satyagraha movement, Gandhi's moral code was elastic. Unfortunately, Gandhi's life was often difficult because he could not accept his human frailties or of those of his wife and children.

While the details of the march were being prepared, Gandhi was invited to meet with the coal mine owners, and he went to Durban to confer with them.

"It is in your hands to bring the strike to an end," Gandhi told the owners.

"We are not government officials," was the reply....

"If you ask the Government to take off the £3 tax, I do think they will refuse to repeal it. You can also educate European opinion on the question.

"But what has the £3 tax to do with the strike?"

Gandhi responded: "I do not see that the labourers have any other weapons except a strike in their hands. The £3 tax too has been imposed in the interest of the mine-owners who want the labourers to work for them but do not wish that they should work as free men...."

"You will not then advise the labourers to return to work?"

"I am sorry I can't."

"Do you know what will be the consequences?"

"I know, I have a full sense of my responsibility."

"Yes, indeed. You have nothing to lose. But will you compensate the misguided labourers for the damage you will cause them?"

"The labourers have gone on strike after due deliberation, and with a full consciousness of the losses which would accrue to them. I cannot conceive a greater loss to a man than the loss of his self-respect, and it is a matter of deep satisfaction to me that the labourers have realized this fundamental principle."

The meeting ended inconclusively, though Gandhi reported that the mine-owners realized their case was weak and that they were communicating with the Government.[7]

Early on the morning of October 28, 1913, the march began. Gandhi could promise only a bare amount of food each day—a pound and a half of bread and one ounce of sugar. The army, with many men carrying blankets on their head and mothers with babies in arms, reached Charlestown on the Transvaal border, safely. The "soldiers" had been instructed to be nonviolent and to bear abuse from Europeans without retaliation.

At Charlestown, a small village, the men marchers were housed on the grounds of a mosque and the women and children were taken to private houses.

The first phase of the march went well, for Gandhi in his service in the Boer War and the Zulu Rebellion, in the establishing of Phoenix and Tolstoy Farm had become skilled in managing complex operations.

At Charlestown, Dr. Briscoe, the District Health Officer, was concerned about the large number of people in the small town of about one thousand inhabitants. Instead of imposing stringent measures to harass this army, Dr. Briscoe made suggestions to Gandhi and offered to help. Gandhi, a true believer in public health, wrote: "Europeans are careful and we are careless about three things, *viz.*, the purity of the water supply, and keeping roads and sanitary conveniences clean."[8] Gandhi accepted all of Dr. Briscoe's suggestions and set an example for the largely uneducated marchers, an example ignored by most leaders throughout the world: he did manual work, including the sweeping and scavenging work of cleaning the premises, roads, and the sanitary facilities. The superiority of being the son of a prime minister are gone. He had declared his lot with the poor.

Sonja Schlesin, with her organizational skills, and Hermann Kallenbach arrived in Charlestown to help with the next phase which did not begin for a few days. Gandhi was in charge of the cooking and serving of meals.

Nonviolence Succeeded but Racism Remained 187

Vegetables and rice were added to the menu while the miners were in Charlestown. The numbers of strikers also grew, for mines away from Newcastle also were closed as the miners worked out and joined the large group there on the Transvaal border.

The next phase of the march, that is, if the authorities did not make mass arrests once the army passed into the Transvaal, was to be eight days. Dr. Briscoe improvised a small medicine chest for Gandhi to use on the road, enough medicines to treat less than a hundred patients, but Gandhi hoped to resupply the medicines from village pharmacies.

And how was bread to be bought? There were no Indian bakers along the route to be travelled, but a European baker in Volksrust, in the Transvaal, contracted to furnish bread, which was shipped by rail. The baker did not take advantage of the marchers and quoted market prices and used excellent ingredients in the bread.[9] The railway officials took good care of the staff of life, for they felt solidarity with the striking workers. Gandhi was calling out the best qualities of Christians, Jews, Hindus, Muslims and others.

Two days before the march began, Europeans in Volksrust held a meeting, making threats that Indians would be shot should they enter the Transvaal. Hermann Kallenbach attended the meeting hoping to reason with them. Several wanted to assault him and one European even challenged him to a duel. Kallenbach responded: "As I have accepted the religion of peace, I may not accept the challenge. Let him who will come and do the worst with me. But I will continue to claim a hearing at this meeting. You have publicly invited all Europeans to attend, and I am here to inform you that not all Europeans are ready as you are to lay violent hands upon innocent men." He went on to say that the charges against Indians were false, and that they sought justice. They were entering the Transvaal not to settle there but to protest the unjust £3 tax. He ended, "They are not the men to beat a retreat from the fear of your bullets or your spears. They propose to melt, and I know they will melt, your hearts by self-suffering." Gandhi reported, no doubt from Kallenbach's report to him, that the audience seemed abashed.[10]

Before the march began, Gandhi made one last attempt to reach a compromise. He telephoned General Smuts's secretary: "Tell General Smuts that I am fully prepared for the march. The Europeans in Volksrust are excited and perhaps likely to violate even the safety of our lives. They have certainly held out such a treat. I am sure that even the General would not wish any such untoward event to happen. If he promises to abolish the £3 tax, I will stop the march, as I will not break the law merely for the sake of breaking it but I am driven to it by inexorable necessity. Will not the General accede to such a small request?"

Within half a minute Gandhi received this message by way of the secretary: "General Smuts will have nothing to do with you. You may do just as you please." Gandhi expected that Smuts would reject the proposal but he was startled by the curtness of the response. Gandhi wrote years later, in *Satyagraha in South Africa*: "But as I would not be elated by his courtesy, I did not weaken in the face of his incivility."[11]

The next day, early, the march began with 2,037 men, 127 women and 57 children.

The crossing into the Transvaal was one mile from Charlestown, and when the marchers reached there they saw a few mounted policemen at the border gate. Gandhi went to speak to the police, leaving word that when he gave a signal the strikers should cross over. While Gandhi was engaged in his talk, the pilgrims made an unexpected movement and crossed the border. The police surrounded those members of the army but made no attempt to arrest anyone. Gandhi took charge, and managed to get them arranged in rows. The march continued. Destination: Tolstoy Farm.

The strikers stopped at Palmford, eight miles from Volksrust, about 5 p.m. and were fed bread and sugar. Early that night Gandhi saw a European, lantern in hand, approaching. The police officer said to him: "I have a warrant of arrest for you. I want to arrest you."

"When?"

"Just now."

"Where will you take me?"

"To the adjoining railway station now, and to Volksrust when we get a train for it."

"I will go with you without informing any one, but I will leave some instructions with one co-worker."

"You may do so."

Gandhi woke P. K. Naidoo to inform him of his arrest and that the pilgrims not be told until the next morning at breakfast time. The march was to continue.[12]

****

The arresting officer was courteous and businesslike. That was not the case with Dr. King's many arrests. In Birmingham, Alabama, on April 12, 1963, Dr. King and his friend Rev. Ralph Abernathy led fifty volunteers on a march. When they came to a police barricade, the marchers came face-to-face with "Bull" Connor. King and Abernathy knelt in prayer and policemen "grabbed them by the seats of their pants and threw them and all the other marchers into paddy wagons...." Taken to jail, Dr. King was placed in solitary confinement.

****

At the court in Volksrust, Gandhi applied for bail and the request was granted. Kallenbach met him with a car, and on the trip back to meet the marchers a reporter from the Transvaal Leader accompanied them, writing a vivid account of the case, the trip, and Gandhi's reuniting with the Satyagrahis.

On the eighth of November, while Gandhi was distributing bread and marmalade, a Magistrate came and stood by Gandhi's side. When the food was distributed, the Magistrate called him aside. Gandhi knew him and thought it was a mere request for a conversation.

Instead, the Magistrate laughed and said, "You are my prisoner."

His sense of humor intact, Gandhi said, "It would seem I have received promotion in rank, as magistrates take the trouble to arrest me instead of mere police officials. But you will try me just now."

"Go with me," the Magistrate said, "the courts are still in session." At the court Gandhi found five of his co-workers had also been arrested. Gandhi once again applied for bail, it was granted, and a carriage returned him to the marchers.[13]

Gokhale wired Gandhi asking that Henry Polak go to India to put before the public and the government the facts of the situation. Polak came to discuss matters with Gandhi, and on November the 9th at 3 p.m., the two were marching at the head of the pilgrims, Polak had planned to leave on the night train.

Mr. Chamney, the Principal Immigration Officer of the Transvaal and a police officer arrived. One said, "I arrest you." The police were abandoning politeness.

"What about the marchers?"

"We will see to that."

Gandhi asked Polak to take charge. The officer allowed Gandhi to tell the marchers that he had been arrested, but as he went on to request that they keep the peace, the officer interrupted. "You are now a prisoner and cannot make any speeches."[14]

Gandhi remained under arrest, was taken to Dundee and charged with inducing laborers to leave Natal and was sentenced to nine months with hard labor.

Polak and Kallenbach were also arrested and sentenced to three months in prison also. Polak could not depart for India as planned.

Gandhi was sent to prison in the Orange Free State. He was the only Indian in prison there, and he was completely isolated from the events being played out in the Transvaal. The medical officer at the prison helped Gandhi receive the fruitarian diet he was then followlng.[15]

Only Sonja Schlesin remained out of jail; she had been working behind the scenes in coordinating the march, and she was fully capable of leading the march. The Transvaal government, after arresting the pilgrims, put them on trains, and returned them to Natal and the coal fields. The prisoners were placed in guarded compounds near the mines, and the government announced that the compounds were outstations of Newcastle and Dundee jails. The European staff of the mine owners were the warders, and the prisoners had become slaves, ordered to get to work. The workers refused and were kicked and abused. Gokhale was fully briefed on what was happening and effectively spread the word in India, and there was great dissatisfaction about this mistreatment of Indians.[16]

Lord Hardinge, the Viceroy in India, entered the controversy in December 1913 and attacked the actions of the Union government and supported the civil disobedients. Praised in India, his strong words were treated adversely in England.[17]

The strike grew well beyond the coal mines, and there were stoppages in sugar cane fields, hotels, restaurants, and other service industries. Soon thousands of additional workers were absent from their jobs. The government of Natal responded by calling in police in an attempt to force the strikers back to work. There were brutal attacks on non-resisters, with broken bones and heads. There were also deaths. The Natal police were using deadly force, which was quickly made known throughout the colonies, India, and England. The outrage could not be ignored in London and Lord Hardinge had carefully stated the Indian response. What to do? Gandhi's analysis is especially important: General Smuts knew that the injustice against Indians needed to be remedied, "but he was in the same predicament as a snake which has made the mouthful of a rat but can neither gulp it down nor cast it out." Smuts needed to do justice, but as a politician he could not. The solution: appoint a commission to do an examination of the matter and make recommendations which would be accepted by the government.[18]

Gandhi, Kallenbach, and Polak were released on December 18, 1913, after six weeks of imprisonment. Three days later, Gandhi spoke at a mass meeting in Durban, dressed as an indentured laborer. At this point his radicalization is almost complete and he has joined the working poor.

Also on December 21, 1913, Gandhi, Kallenbach, and Polak wrote to Smuts welcoming the three-person committee but objecting that two of the members disliked Indians and asking for some impartial men also join the work of the committee. Smuts refused, but Gandhi and friends need not have worried. The arrangements had been made for the committee to make findings agreeable to Gandhi and the Indian protestors. The recommendations would give cover to Smuts and his government and would be passed.[19] Prisoners were released and Satyagraha stopped, awaiting the decision.

Gandhi did not seem to recognize that the fix was in and continued to raise questions about the make-up of the commission. Gandhi did one thing during this time that put him and the Satyagrahi movement in a favorable light with the government. European railroad workers went on strike, but Gandhi announced that Indians would not support those strikers because the movement was different and he did not wish to harass the government. His lack of solidarity with railway strikers, though, is troubling.

The commission published its report on March 7, 1914.

Recommendations:

Nonviolence Succeeded but Racism Remained

Repeal of the £3 tax

Legalization of marriages according to the rites of Hinduism, Islam, etc.

Rights of bona fide former residents.[20]

In May and June of 1914 both houses of the South African Parliament passed the Indian Relief Act, including the three recommendations above.[21]

Items of special interest to Indian merchants were not specifically addressed in the formal agreement. Gandhi had originally sought admission of "exempted" educated Indians to enter the country. That was covered by correspondence between Gandhi and Smuts, Smuts agreeing that existing laws would be administered "in a just manner and with due regard to vested rights." Smuts was not trustworthy, and his agreement in a letter suspect. Merchants still could not own land, reside, or do business in some parts of the country. Many rich Indian businessmen had grown tired of the conflict, were reluctant to go to jail, and resented Gandhi's emphasis on helping the poorest of the poor Indians. Gandhi's new alignment with the poor was evident in his dress. He now wore the clothes of indentured workers.

In the long struggle in South Africa, Gandhi learned to be a tactician.[22] Against all odds, he rallied Indians to a nonviolent protest against the injustices they faced. Without his actions, Indians would have been hounded out of that country—and probably ejected from other colonies where they were indentured laborers. He learned, and perfected, a methodology which he then took to India to bring about the ouster of the Raj.

At the end of the Satyagraha struggle, Tolstoy Farm lost its settlers, but Phoenix was still in operation. Several members of the Gandhi family were there including Mrs. Gandhi and their twenty-one year old son Manilal.

In July of 1913, Gandhi was in Johannesburg, and as he wrote in his *Autobiography*, "he received tidings of the moral fall of two of the inmates of the Ashram." What Gandhi did learn was that his son Manilal was having a sexual affair with a married woman. Upon learning this, Gandhi was in a terrible state and Kallenbach insisted on accompanying him on the train to Phoenix. To make the guilty parties aware of his distress and also the enormity of their own fall, he decided to do penance. He would fast for seven days and then have only one meal a day for the next four and a half months. Kallenbach tried to convince his friend not to undertake this penance, failed, then joined the penance.[23]

Gandhi caused himself much pain and suffering by refusing to acknowledge human frailty. During the 1913 march, he was aware that some of the pilgrims and been jailed for murder, adultery, or theft, but he did not consider himself fit to sit in judgment over the morality of the strikers. He would have saved the entire Gandhi family much turmoil if he had taken the same attitude toward his son and the married woman. Gandhi was unwilling to recognize the effects of his puritanical sexual views on his twenty-one year old son.

The dramatic 1913 march organized by Gandhi was peaceful. Over two thousand mostly poor Indians marched through the countryside, unafraid of being arrested and sent to jail. The government of South Africa wanted Indians as workers on farms, in hotels and restaurants, and in mines but wished to keep them in segregated peonage. Indian merchants were a danger to the profits of European merchants. The march was a signal that Indians were demanding their rights as members of the British Empire.

****

Dr. King's followers were also mostly poor, and they had grown up in a racist, segregated society. The local and state government officials were prone to use violence against protestors and marchers.

In 1965, Dr. King was in Selma, Alabama, leading a voting rights campaign. The opposition was led by Sheriff Jim Clark. Various ploys were used to keep African Americans from registering to vote; in one line of aspiring voters, snakes were thrown on them. Once inside the office they had to answer questions that would have baffled Ph.D.s in political science.

On February 10, 1965, the sheriff's men attacked a group of young student marchers, hitting them and using electric cattle prods. "You want to march, didn't you" the sheriff's men called, "Now march." The posse chased the young people for about a mile until they stumbled into ditches, crying and vomiting.

Dr. King then led a protest of two thousand eight hundred African Americans, vowing that they were going to bring a voting rights bill into being. At the Selma courthouse, Sheriff Clark used a billy club to hit C. T. Vivian, one of Dr. King's aides, in the stomach. Vivian tried to take that club away, only to be hit in the mouth by a billy club swung by a deputy. Reporters were taking notes on this violent scene, and the television cameras were rolling. *Time* succinctly reported that the sheriff was the anti-segregation movement's energizing force, for every time it faltered, Clark and his deputies managed to revive it with some new outrage.[24]

****

The last weeks in South Africa must have been bittersweet for Gandhi. The nonviolence campaign was bringing great benefits to Indians there, but he must have known from his twenty years there that most European inhabitants did not suddenly give up their racist views. The British government, he had finally learned, would publicly declare that all members of the Empire, whatever their race, color, or religion, would granted their full rights but surreptitiously supporting racism at the same time. He could see that his ideas were appealing to the poor. Though he made many efforts, he was not overcome the old animosities of Hindus, Muslims, and Christians.

****

Dr. King did not live to see the promised land. In fact, the promised land, for all the changes he helped bring about, is for many minorities and for poor people of all races, still a dream, often nightmarish.

****

The Gandhis were ready to leave South Africa forever, but before their departure Mrs. Gandhi became seriously ill. The exact nature of her declining health was never specified. On March 1, 1914, Gandhi wrote Kallenbach that Mrs. Gandhi wanted medicine in the mildest form "and she is now laid up with fever, aches all over and pain in the stomach." Gandhi thought death would be a deliverance for her.[25] On March 9, 1914, Gandhi wrote Kallenbach that Mrs. Gandhi was recovering, and surely a miracle, for he feared for her life and "had made arrangements for her funeral."[26] There are hints that some of her problem was caused by hysteria.

The bitter quarrel between the Gandhis began on about April 11, 1914 and was first about Jaykunvar (called Jeki), who was staying with the Gandhis. She was the daughter of Gandhi's close friend Dr. Mehta, who gave financial support to the movement. Jeki was married to Manilal Doctor, a barrister, then in Fiji, and the two seem to have been estranged at this time. Jeki may have been the married woman Manilal Gandhi had an affair with, mentioned earlier in this chapter. In the spring of 1914, Manilal Gandhi was being kept away from Jeki and was in Kallenbach's care. Gandhi told Kallenbach on May 13, 1914, that Manilal was infatuated with Jeki and called her a "liar, a wretched hypocrite, without pity, without remorse, full of evil passions."[27] Mrs. Gandhi appears to have disliked Jeki even more than her husband did, probably believing Jeki had seduced her son.

In a letter of April 12, 1914, Gandhi told Kallenbach how to read the events of the previous day: Mrs. Gandhi was better but in her actions yesterday "once more proved what I have told you, namely, that she has both the devil and the divine in her in a most concentrated form."

She began with a venomous remark: "Who has opened Devadas's drawer?" suggesting that Jeki had tampered with it." (Mrs. Gandhi may have thought Jeki had designs on their son Devadas.)

Mrs. Gandhi "spit fire" in her comments on Jeki.

Gandhi "gently" told her he had opened the drawer.

"Why?"

"In order to see whether I could find a sheet for you."

"That does not contain sheets," Mrs. Gandhi felt Gandhi was lying to protect Jeki.

He then "gently but rebukingly" told his wife "that she was sinful in her thought; and that her disease was largely due to her sins." Provoked, she said he had forbidden good food to her to make her die, that he was tired of her and wished her to die. Gandhi told Kallenbach that her remarks were "vicious," but they did ring partly true to readers of this letter. He had forced diets on her, had forced her to give up sexual activities, and had arranged her funeral (probably, being truthful, told her he had done so). Not surprising, she began to "howl."

Gandhi noted, without being aware of any complicity in Mrs. Gandhi's emotional problems, that his "love has not been sufficiently intense and selfless to make her change her nature." He did not think she had been a bad wife, and he recognized that no other woman would have accepted the changes forced upon her. She had taught him the "emptiness of the world." He asserted a belief he often expressed: "you cannot attach yourself to a particular woman and live for humanity."[28]

It is difficult not to come to the conclusion that Gandhi did not love his wife in any meaningful way. Although Kallenbach hankered for Gandhi's affection and was jealous of others who were close to Gandhi, he did bring some peace and quiet into the life of his soul mate. Moreover, he brought love, which was reciprocated.

Somehow, we must try to understand this part of Gandhi's life. Two incompatible children were married. Emotionally, Gandhi was more attracted to men than to women. As he became a revolutionary for nonviolent protest, his wife and children suffered. He is now seen as one of the most notable and admired men in human history, for he found ways to oppose widespread racism and its effects. This Gandhian movement was adopted by Dr. Martin Luther, King, Jr., for the American scene.

Gandhi is now a mythic figure, celebrated for his deep religious underpinning and for Satyagraha; his large-scale human foibles and mistakes are largely forgotten. His life, his wish for national independence from foreigners, his desire for peace and religious harmony have an appeal to peoples around the world. In our materialistic age, his call for a simplified life resonates, just as Thoreau's does in *Walden*, even though such a life seems to flourish only in our dreams. Few leaders have been concerned for the poor and dispossessed as he was. In many parts of the world, there are eruptions of Satyagraha, some successful, some brutally suppressed, and racism and discrimination remain in many parts of the world. Nonviolent civil disobedients, with the optimism of Gandhi, have attempted to overthrow dictators, tyrants, and foreign rulers and to give basic human rights to the masses.

Until the end of his life, Gandhi fought against racism. He often failed, but he continued his efforts. The 1913–1914 settlement in South Africa turned out to be short lived, and non-whites in that country had to endure several more decades of racism. For his efforts, he has become universally known as Mahatma (a wise and holy man). Dr. King, who built on Gandhi's Satyagraha movement, is also honored worldwide.

Notes

1. Gandhi, *Satyagraha in South Africa*, pp. 428–36.
2. Oates, *Let the Trumpet Sound*, pp. 225–27; Martin Luther King, Jr., *Autobiography*, pp. 205–11.
3. Gandhi, *Satyagraha in South Africa*, pp. 434–38.
4. Rajmohan Gandhi, *Mohandas*, p.175.
5. Gandhi, *Satyagraha in South Africa*, pp. 438–39.
6. Ibid., pp. 434–41.
7. Ibid., pp 442–44.
8. Ibid., pp. 445–50.
9. Ibid., pp. 451–55.
10. Ibid., pp. 458.
11. Ibid., p. 456.
12. Ibid., pp. 459–60.
13. Ibid., pp. 462–63.
14. Ibid., p 466.
15. Ibid., pp. 464–74.
16. Ibid., pp. 474–75.
17. Ibid., p. 477.
18. Ibid., p. 485.
19. Ibid., p. 485–88.
20. Ibid., p. 499.
21. bid, pp. 494–508.
22. Rajmohan Gandhi, *Mohandas*, p. 182.
23. Gandhi, *Autobiography*, p. 418; Rajmohan Gandhi, *Mohandas*, pp. 183–84.
24. Martin Luther King, Jr., *Autobiography*, pp. 270–83; Oates, *Let the Trumpet Sound*, p. 334.
25. Gandhi, *Collected Works*, 96:168.
26. Ibid., 96:171.
27. Ibid., 96:188–89.
28. Ibid., 96:181–82.

BIBLIOGRAPHY

Blassingame, John W. *Slave Testimony*. Baton Rouge: Louisiana State University Press, 1977.

Branch, Taylor. *Parting the Waters: America in the King Years, 1954–1963*. New York: Simon and Schuster, 1988.

Brinkley, Douglas. *Rosa Parks*. New York: Viking, 2000.

Christy, Arthur C. *The Orient in American Transcendentalism*. New York: Columbia University Press, 1932.

Doke, Joseph J. *M. K. Gandhi: An Indian Patriot in South Africa*. Madras: G. A. Natesan & Co., n. d.

Dray, Philip. *At the Hands of Persons Unknown: The Lynching of Black America*. New York: Random House, 2002.

Erikson, Erik H. *Gandhi's Truth: On the Origins of Militant Nonviolence*. New York: W. W. Norton & Company, 1969.

Fischer, Louis, *The Life of Mahatma Gandhi*. New York: Harper & Brothers, 1950.

Franklin, John Hope and Alfred A. Moss, Jr. *From Slavery to Freedom*. New York: Alfred A. Knopf, 2003.

Fredrlckson, George M. *Black Liberation*. New York: Oxford University Press, 1995.

Gandhi, M. K. *Autobiography: The Story of My Experiments with Truth*. Washington, D. C.: Public Affairs Press, 1948.

———. *The Collected Works of Mahatma Gandhi*. New Delhi: Publications Division, 1958–.

———. *The Gospel of Selfless Action, or, The Gita According to Gandhi*. Ahmedabad: Navajivan Publishing Co., 1946.

———. *Indian Home Rule or Hind Swaraj*. Madras: G.A. Natesan & Co., Sixth edition, n. d.

———. *Satyagraha in South Africa*. Ahmedabad: Navajivan Publishing House, 1928.

Gandhi, Rajmohan, *Mohandas: A True Story of a Man, His People and an Empire*. New York: Penguin, 2006.

Gilmour, David, *The Ruling Caste*. New York: Farrar, Straus and Giroux, 2005.

Green, Martin. *Gandhi*. Mount Jackson, Virginia: Axios Press, n. d.

Hendrick, George and Willene Hendrick. *Black Refugees in Canada*. Jefferson, North Carolina: McFarland & Co., 2010.

Hendrick, George. *Henry Salt: Humanitarian Reformer and Man of Letters*. Urbana: University of Illinois Press, 1977.

Hendrick, George and Willene Hendrick. *Why Not Every Man? African Americans and Civil Disobedience in the Quest for the Dream*. Chicago: Ivan R. Dee, 2005.

Henson, Josiah. *Father Henson's Story of His Own Life*. Boston: John P. Jewett & Company, 1858.

Hine, Darlene Clark, William C. Hine, and Stanley Harrold. *The African-American Odyssey*. Upper Saddle River, New Jersey: Prentice Hall, 2000.

Hunt, James D. *Gandhi and the Nonconformists: Encounters in South Africa*. New Delhi: Promilla & Co., 1986.

———. *Gandhi in London*. New Delhi: Promilla & Co., 1978.

Huttenback, Robert A. *Gandhi in South Africa*. Ithaca: Cornell University Press, 1971.

King, Martin Luther, Jr. *Autobiography*, ed. by Clayborne Carson. New York: Warner Books, 1998.

———. *Stride Toward Freedom*. New York: Harper & Brothers, 1958.

Lelyveld, Joseph. *Great Soul: Mahatma Gandhi and His Struggle with India*. New York: Alfred A. Knopf, 2011.

Lewis, David L. *King: A Biography*. Urbana: University of Illinois Press, 1978.

Bibliography

Loewen, James. *Sundown Towns. A Hidden Dimension of American Racism*. New York: New Press, 2005.

Mann, Robert James, ed. *The Colony of Natal. An Account of the Characteristics and Capabilities of the British Dependency. Published under the Authority of the Government Immigration Board, for the Guidance and Information of Emigrants*. London: Jerrold and Sons, [1859].

McFeely, William S. *Frederick Douglass*. New York: Norton, 1991.

Nag, Kalidas. *Tolstoy and Gandhi*. Patna: Pustak Bhandar, 1950.

Oates, Stephen B. *Let the Trumpet Sound: The Life of Martin Luther King, Jr*. New York: New American Library, 1982.

Oehlschlaeger, Fritz and George Hendrick. *Toward the Making of Thoreau's Modern Reputation*. Urbana: University of Illinois Press, 1979.

Parks, Rosa. *Quiet Strength*. Grand Rapids, Michigan: Zondervan Publishing House, 1994.

Payne, Robert. *The Life and Death of Mahatma Gandhi*. New York: E. P. Dutton & Co., 1969.

Polak, Millie Graham. *Mr. Gandhi the Man*. Bombay: Vora & Co., 1950.

Pyarelal. *The Early Phase*. Ahmedabad: Navajivan Publishing Company, 1965.

Ruskin, John. *Unto This Last: A Paraphrase*. Translated by Gandhi in Gujarati, appearing in *Indian Opinion*, beginning May, 1908. Retranslated into English. Ahmedabad: Navajivan Publishing House, 1951.

Smith, Warren Sylvester. *The London Heretics, 1870–1914*. New York: Dodd, Mead & Company, 1968.

Tendulkar, D. G. *Mahatma*. Vol I. Bombay: The Times of India, 1951.

Thoreau, Henry David. *Walden*. Dozens of editions.

Winsten, Stephen. *Salt and His Circle*. London: Hutchinson & Co., 1951.

INDEX

Abbott, Anderson Ruffin, 103
Abbott, Wilson Ruffin, 72
Abernathy, Ralph, 189
Alam, Mir, 153, 155–157, 160, 163
Alexander, Mrs., 83, 91–92
Alexander, Superintendent, 83, 85–87, 91, 158
Alfred High School, 3, 6, 100
Ali, Hajer Ojer, 143–144
Arnold, Sir Edwin, 23–24, 49
Asiatic Act, 147, 153, 168
Augusta, Dr. A. T., 61

Baker, A. W., 48–49, 88, 187
Baker, Frazier B., 88
Balasundaram (Tamil indentured laborer), 62
Besant, Annie, 24, 26
Bhagavad-Gita, 2, 9, 23, 149
Bible, 25, 48, 152
Black Act (anti-Indian ordinance), 130, 143–145, 147, 149–150, 152, 158, 175
black laws in northern states, xiv, 74, 111, 144
Blavatsky, Mme., 24
Boer War, 101, 104, 110–111, 114, 155, 186
Botha, General, 168
Bradburn, George, 83
Bradlaugh, Charles, 26
Brickfields (Johannesburg ghetto), 120–121
Briscoe, Dr., 186–187
Brown v. Board of Education, 74

bubonic plague
 in Bombay, 79
 in Johannesburg, 120

Cape (South African colony), 36, 49, 72, 175, 177, 181
caste system, 13
Cartwright, Albert, 152
Chamberlain, Joseph (Secretary of State for the Colonies), xvii, 89, 95–96, 101–102, 110–112, 134, 137, 141, 179
Charlestown (in South Africa), 43, 186–188
Clark, Jim, 194
Colonial Patriotic Union, 77
Coates, Michael, 49
Connor, Eugene ("Bull"), 127, 183, 189
Crisis, The (journal of NAACP), 112, 120

Dick, Miss, 118
Doctor, Jaykunvar ("Jeki," née Mehta), 18, 83, 99, 106, 157, 169, 174, 196
Doke, J. J., 156–158, 171
 biography of Gandhi, 170, 179
Douglass, Frederick, 40, 44, 83, 91, 94, 96, 114
Dredd Scott (Supreme Court decision), 177
DuBois, W. E. B., 120

Durban, xiv, 37–40, 52, 64, 66, 74, 77–81, 83, 89, 102, 110, 112, 122–123, 129, 158, 185, 192

Eisenhower, Dwight. D., 74
Elgin, Lord (Secretary of State for the Colonies), 143–144, 148
Escombe, Harry, 52, 60, 80–81
Erikson, Erik
    Gandhi's Truth, 7, 15–16, 42, 55

Faubus, Orville, 74

Gandhi, Devadas, ix–x, xii, xiv–xvii, 1–55, 57–67, 69–83, 85–87, 89–115, 117–126, 128–135, 137–141, 143–153, 155–163, 165–177, 179–199
Gandhi, Harilal, ix–x, xii, xiv–xvii, 1–55, 57–67, 69–83, 85–87, 89–115, 117–126, 128–135, 137–141, 143–153, 155–163, 165–177, 179–199
Gandhi, Kasturba (wife, née Kapadia), 4, 6–10, 12–13, 16, 26, 32–33, 105
Gandhi, Kaba (Karamchand), 1–3, 9
Gandhi, Karsandas (brother), 4, 8
Gandhi, Laxmidas (brother), 8, 10, 12–13, 16, 31–36, 145, 174
Gandhi, Manilal (son), 109–110, 193–194, 196

Gandhi, Mohandas K.
    Autobiography, xvii, 2, 4, 6–9, 15–16, 23–24, 27, 29–30, 32–33, 37–38, 41, 51, 54–55, 64–67, 78, 93–94, 97, 99, 101, 109, 114–115, 125–126, 128, 134, 138, 170, 179, 194, 199
    early education of, 174
    education of children, 97–98, 100, 124, 129–130
    flirtation with unnamed woman in London, 28
    Green Pamphlet, 70–71, 74–77, 81, 89, 93
    Indian Home Rule or Hind Swaraj, 97, 114, 168, 176, 179
    in Bombay (Mumbai), 1, 10, 12, 14, 16, 18, 22, 31–34, 37, 52, 70, 74, 76, 108, 110, 121
    in Rajkot, 1, 3, 8, 13, 16, 25, 31–34, 36, 64, 70, 75–76, 100, 106–108, 145
    in South Africa, xii, xiv–xv, xvii, 1, 7, 9, 11, 17, 22–23, 31–32, 36–37, 39, 42, 49–51, 54, 58, 62–63, 66, 69–71, 73–75, 77–79, 92, 94, 96, 98–99, 101–104, 106, 110, 114–115, 118, 121–122, 130, 132, 134–135, 137–138, 140, 144, 146, 151, 155, 160, 162–163, 166–168, 170–171, 175–177, 179–182, 184, 188, 193–196, 198–199
    jailed, 150, 171, 176, 194
    public health issues, 76, 106, 172, 186

Index

Gandhi, Mohandas K.
  segregated travel, 46
  service during Boer War,
    101–102, 104, 110, 114, 155,
    186
  service during Zulu Rebellion,
    126, 128, 186
  studies bookkeeping, 39, 51
  studies Indian languages, 69
  views on animal sacrifice, 107
  views on animal rights, 20, 108
  views on religion, 9, 12–13, 23,
    25, 48–49, 57, 63, 70, 108,
    146, 172, 195
  views on sexuality, 7, 170, 173
Gandhi, Ramdas, 98
Gayle, W. A., 90
Gokhale, Gopal Krishna, 75

Habid, Sheth Haji, 131
Hardinge, Lord (Viceroy of India), 191
Henson, Josiah, 11, 16

Immigration Restriction Act, 168
indentured labor (in South Africa), xiii
Indian franchise bill, 52
Indian Opinion, 117, 119–120,
  122–123, 129–130, 145–146,
  148, 150–151, 158

Jeki *see* Doctor, Jaykunvar
Jhaveri, Sheth Abdul Karim, 36–37
Jones, A. T., 29, 63

Kallenbach, Hermann, 117, 137,
  171, 186–187
Kachhalia, A. M., 159
Keightley, Archibald, 23
Keightley, Bertram, 23

King, Dr. Martin Luther, Jr., xii,
  xiv–xvii, 41, 90–91, 130,
  132, 150–152, 160, 166, 169,
  179, 182–183, 189, 194–196,
  198–199
Ku Klux Klan, xi

Lazarus, D., 183
Lely, Frederick, 10
Lelyveld, Joseph
  Great Soul, xvii, 134, 137, 141,
    179
Lincoln, Abraham, 103
Lincoln, Robert Todd, 103
Little, John, 127
Litton, Brute, 11
London Times, 58
Lynching, 69, 88–89, 94–95

Mahatma (title meaning "great
  soul"), xvii, 134, 137, 141, 179
Maritzburg, 40–42
Mazmudar, Tryambakrai, 17
Mehta, Dr. P. J., 18
Mehta, Sir Pherozeshah, 35
Mehtab, Sheikh, 4, 64
Morgan, Juliette, 159

Naidoo, P. K., 189
Natal (province), xii–xiii, xvii,
  36–39, 42, 45, 52, 57, 59–62,
  71, 74, 76–77, 79–81, 85–86, 89,
  95–96, 110, 126, 151, 165, 176,
  182, 190–191
Natal Indian Congress, 61–62, 110
Natal Mercury, 71
Newcastle (in South Africa), 182,
  184, 187, 191
Nixon, E. D., 132
Nonviolence, 8, 84–85, 102, 150,
  170–171, 181–183, 195

Oldfield, Josiah, 26
Ollivant, E. C. K., 34
Orange Free State, xiii, 36, 52, 73, 78, 191

Palmford (city in South Africa), 188
Parks, Rosa, xv, 41, 54, 58–59, 67, 90, 130–131, 159
Perry, Benjamin F., xi
Plessy v. Fergusson, 71
Phoenix Farm, 126, 171
Polak, Henry, 118, 121, 146, 190
Polak, Millie (née Graham), 124, 134
poll taxes, xi, 58
Pretoria, 39, 41–42, 45–47, 50–52, 111–112, 153

Raj (British rule in India), ix–x, 2, 5, 11, 25, 35–36, 168–170, 193
Rajchandra, 32, 75, 98
Reconstruction (United States), xi, 58, 63, 87
Reuters (news agency), 76–77
Riley, Isaac, 11
Ripon, Lord (Robinson, George, Secretary of State for the Colonies), 58
Ritch, Louis, 119
Ruskin, John, 20, 122–123, 134, 152
Rustomji, 82–83, 85–87, 99, 158

Salt, Henry, 19, 22, 29, 149, 162
Satyagraha movement, xvii, 54, 94, 101, 113–115, 120, 134–135, 138, 145, 150, 155, 160, 162–163, 165, 167–168, 170–171, 176–177, 179–180, 184, 188, 192–193, 198–199

Schlesin, Sonja, 118, 176, 182, 186, 191
Scott, Dredd, 177
Searle, Justice (Malcolm), 165, 177, 181
Segregation, vii, xii, xiv–xv, 40, 42, 58, 90, 131–132, 150, 166, 182, 195
Sellers, Clyde, 90
Shadd, Dr. Furman Jeremiah, 61
Sharecropping, xiv
Sheth, Abdulla, 38–39, 42, 52–53
Sheth, Tayeb, 36–39, 42, 44–46, 52–53, 131
Shukla, Dalpatram, 18
Stowe, Harriet Beecher, 11
Smiley, C. T., 90
Smuts, Jan, 143, 152–154, 158, 160, 175–176, 188, 191–193
Solomon, Sir Richard, 144
sundown towns, 73, 93

Taney, Roger B., 177
theosophy, 23–24, 48
Thoreau, Henry David, 147, 149
Tilak, Bal Gangadhar, 76
Times of India, 58, 77
Tolstoy, Leo, 20, 50, 63, 118, 122–123, 138, 152, 170–174, 176, 179, 182, 184, 186, 188, 193
Tolstoy Farm, 138, 172–174, 176, 179, 182, 184, 186, 188, 193
Transvaal, xiii, 36, 39, 43, 45, 48, 50, 73, 78, 95, 101, 110–113, 118–119, 124, 131, 143–147, 152, 155, 158–159, 161, 165, 167, 170–171, 182, 184, 186–191

Vivian, C.T., 195

Volksraad (Transvaal legislative assembly), 77
Volksrust (cit in South Africa), 166, 187–189
Victoria, Queen (and Empress of India), ix, 11

West, Albert, 122–123
White, William, 84, 91

Zulu Rebellion, 126, 128, 186

About the Authors

George Hendrick is Professor Emeritus of English, University of Illinois at Urbana-Champaign. Previously he held the Chair of American Studies at J. W. Goethe Universität, Frankfurt am Main. He is the editor and author of many books on Thoreau, Katherine Anne Porter, Sandburg, and on African-American topics. His late wife, Willene was the co-author of many of these books.

Willene Hendrick (1928–2010) was a nurse for thirty-eight years. Upon her retirement from Planned Parenthood, she began a second career as a writer and editor. With her husband, she published such works as *Fleeing for Freedom: Stories of the Underground Railroad* and *Selected Poems of Carl Sandburg*.

www.ingramcontent.com/pod-product-compliance
Lightning Source LLC
Chambersburg PA
CBHW022006160426
43197CB00007B/300